The Negative Imagination

FORM AND PERSPECTIVE IN THE
NOVELS OF HENRY JAMES

The Negative Imagination

FORM AND PERSPECTIVE IN THE
NOVELS OF HENRY JAMES

Sallie Sears

Cornell University Press ⁎ ITHACA, NEW YORK

First published 1968

Library of Congress Catalog Card Number: 68–9754

PRINTED IN THE UNITED STATES OF AMERICA
BY THE VAIL-BALLOU PRESS, INC.

For Georgianna Lord

Contents

	Preface	ix
I	Perspective and Form	1
II	*The Wings of the Dove*	59
III	*The Ambassadors*	99
IV	*The Golden Bowl*	153
	Bibliography	223
	Index of Names and Titles	229

Preface

THIS WORK has its beginning in the observation
that James characteristically polarized the structures of
his imaginative world, establishing them as oppositions, as
extremes that could not meet, as equally desirable yet
mutually exclusive possibilities for life. The choices open
to the characters, for example, are severely limited: they
are placed in situations in which the selection of one thing
means a blanket loss of other alternatives. At the same
time, they are all the sort of people for whom compromise
is extraordinarily difficult—good and bad alike, they tend
to define happiness as having everything, all alternatives,
all possibilities. Their impulses protest against the very
notions of selectivity, necessity, inevitability. They are
people who to an unusual degree reject limitations, yet

they must function in contexts that are unusually limiting. It is out of these two tensions that the dramatic conflict in the novels arises, out of a force working to close in upon and barricade experience and a force pushing out to explode it, in defiance of all barriers. The first manifests itself in the severity of the circumstances the characters find themselves in, the second in the characters' passionate resistance to these very circumstances that threaten to mutilate their chances for happiness. In both of these phenomena there is an element of exaggeration: the terms of reality are more limited, the defiance of the terms more intense, than we ordinarily find in life.

The Jamesian hero in his resistance typically balks at the either-or nature of the choices confronting him: wanting to go for broke, he tries to create a new reality that will have different, more pleasing premises. In this attempt he is often enough assisted by some other character for whom his acceptance of an illusion is an advantage—or so at least the antagonist believes.

Also typically, both are wrong. The terms, the stringent condition of things, in most cases cannot be changed; when they can, the change exacts so severe a penalty that both hero and villain find the universe of their wishes, when realized (as in the fairy-tale archetype), so much more dreadful than the one they left behind that they can only spend their last wish on the restitution of things the way they were before. But as is not true of the fairy tale, there is no exit from the intricately constructed but empty and terrifying universe that the Jamesian characters create for themselves.

In a certain sense, it may be said that when brought into conjunction the individual illusions—their own imaginary worlds—that the characters create for themselves annihilate each other. They cannot coexist because the victory of one *by definition* means the undoing of the other, though at first the opposite appears to be the case: to survive, it seems, they must have each other, are indeed the very condition of each other's existence. (Think, for example, of how the fantasies of both Osmond and Isabel seem so neatly and absolutely realized by their union; or what the Ververs on the one hand and the Prince and Charlotte on the other believe they have found in each other.)

The process of annihilation is not instantaneous but slow, intricate, and elaborate: a vast architectonics of destruction. Only when the last piece is in place—which means when the last illusion has been stripped away—and the edifice stands complete, is it revealed as a house of pain and death; in a certain sense, a nonworld.

This process, of the creation, collision, and destruction of fictions has, as I shall try to show in the first chapter, its analogue in James's treatment of language and both are rooted in a lifelong skepticism, which, in turn, I believe (though I have no interest in proselytizing on the matter), is related—for James—to an unresolvable and permanent ambivalence toward existence itself.

Where James could achieve "integrity"—wholeness— was in artistic form: each piece of his designs seems to fit diabolically with every other to lead to the inevitable woe. And so a tension is established in his works between the "certainty" of the patterning of events and the uncertainty of the significance of both terms and events. What is unclear in his novels is not so much (except in *The Sacred Fount*) what happens as what we are to make of it, how we are to understand, evaluate, literally apprehend it.

The final chapters, which deal with some of the consequences of this tension, represent an effort to describe the form James's negative imagination took in his late fiction and to articulate some of its literary consequences. Each of the last novels can be looked upon as an unresolved debate about the promise and meaning of life, a debate between a voice of yearning and a voice of restriction. Whatever James saw that seemed potentially beautiful had a kind of built-in abortive principle to it, contained the seeds of its own doom. I have called this vision "negative" rather than "tragic" in part because James could not assert positive values with any degree of success of conviction.[1] He could not, though he spent his life trying, resolve the conflict of feeling that characterizes and dictates the ordering of his fictional worlds. The first chapter examines one work (*The Europeans*) from James's early period and one (*What Maisie Knew*) from the later period of the so-called "problem novels." *The Europeans* is one of the few works in which James seems to have achieved a partial triumph of positive values. But, as we shall see, the victory is illusory and is built upon an undermining of his own language, so that the very words that establish the conflict are redefined in the course of the novel to the point where the "conflict," rather than being solved, simply evaporates.

[1] As F. O. Matthiessen has pointed out, James's characteristic themes are those of "deprivation, of loss, of lack of fulfillment," just as his characteristic values are those of resignation and renunciation. *Henry James: The Major Phase* (New York, 1944), p. 51.

This process of redefinition—of assigning a key term ("American" or "evil," for example) first one meaning and then another (often enough the opposite of the first), which eventually in his career involves presenting reality from multifarious perspectives—becomes radical in *What Maisie Knew,* as it certainly is in *The Golden Bowl.* It is among the things that make James one of the early modern novelists, involving as it does an overthrow of some of the profoundest complacencies of the language, and hence of the consciousness, of the past.

SALLIE SEARS

New York City
May, 1968

The Negative Imagination
FORM AND PERSPECTIVE IN THE
NOVELS OF HENRY JAMES

CHAPTER I

Perspective and Form

A PREOCCUPATION—even obsession—with defeat, loss, renunciation was to persist throughout James's career, attended by an unreconcilable yearning for almost utopian gratification. The relationship between these two concerns became extremely complex in his middle and late works; it was less so in the earlier ones. In *The American,* for example, the two can be seen in rather bold relief. The novel's hero, Christopher Newman, wants everything and (other than some bad copies of paintings for which he has been overcharged) ends up with nothing. He has arrived in Europe seeking, he says, "the biggest kind of entertainment a man can get. People, places, art, nature, everything! I want to see the tallest mountains, and the bluest lakes, and . . .

the most celebrated men, and the most elegant women." [1]

In particular, Newman wants "a great woman," someone "as good as she's beautiful and as clever as she's good. . . . I want, in a word, the best article in the market. . . . When I say rare I mean rare all through— grown as a rarity and recognized as one. . . . I want the best thing going" (49–50).

It seems at first that he is going to get what he wants; then he is completely undermined.[2] When James came to write the Preface to the novel some twenty years later, it was "difficult" for him "to believe" that at the time he was composing it he had not known, had not at least *some shade of the rueful sense of [his] affront to verisimilitude*" [3] entailed in the Bellegardes' rejection of Newman, and he pointed out that they "would positively have jumped . . . at my rich and easy American, and not have 'minded' in the least any drawback." His explanation indicates an overriding preoccupation, one that he was to handle more skillfully later on: "I was so possessed of my idea that Newman be ill-used—which was the essence of my subject—that I attached too scant an importance to its fashion of coming about." [4]

[1] New York ed., Vol. II (New York, 1907), p. 33.

[2] For those not familiar with this novel, Newman, a businessman who is rich enough to indulge his fantasy of procuring the "best," finds his "perfect" woman—Claire de Bellegarde, descended from "fabulous antiquity" (53) of French and English aristocracy. Her family at first accepts Newman's suit for Claire's hand and then recants (though they need money) on the grounds that they simply can't tolerate the idea of a "commercial person" in the family. Newman relinquishes a chance for revenge, but is inwardly undone. Claire joins a nunnery.

[3] *The Art of the Novel: Critical Prefaces,* ed. R. P. Blackmur (New York, 1962), p. 37.

[4] *Ibid.,* p. 35.

The concern with defeat seems submerged in James's next novel, *The Europeans: A Sketch* (1878), which is one of the few works of his that ends at least somewhat happily.[5] With the exception of the Baroness's final plight, the book is built out of stock comic elements: lovers who are ill paired but sort out properly at the end after confusions, misunderstandings, and near misses; the triumph of young love over the resistant, conservative, parental world; the undermining of arrogant piety; the intrusion of some complicating element (here, the arrival of the Baroness and Felix) into a scene of relative calm, the ensuing complication, and the restoration of final calm.

The novel establishes an initial opposition, characteristic of James, between pleasure and morality. Like Strether's Woollett, Massachusetts (which "isn't sure it

---

[5] (London, 1952.) The text of this edition is taken from that of the Uniform Edition published between 1921 and 1923. (This novel was not included in the New York Edition of 1907–1909.) All subsequent citations from *The Europeans* are to this edition.

In this work, the Baroness Eugenia-Camillia-Dolores-Münster comes with her brother, Felix Young, to New England from Europe to stay with some wealthy American cousins, the Wentworths, in hopes of making her fortune. The Baroness, who has considerable style though not beauty (or rectitude), is ultimately rejected because of her amorality by a wealthy bachelor, Mr. Robert Acton. Felix and Gertrude Wentworth, the "problem daughter" of the family, fall in love and their union finally succeeds in spite of a variety of obstacles such as her family's wish to have her marry Mr. Brand, a stuffy young minister, for the sake of her character. Since it is impossible not to be sympathetic with the Baroness (who has flair and is much more interesting than any of the Americans), we may say the novel ends "half happily." The divided ending—one protagonist "winning," the other "losing"—is significant, as we shall see, and is an uncharacteristic resolution in the comic genre.

ought to enjoy. If it were it would"), this little society (also Massachusetts) is dubious about pleasure:

"We are not fond of amusement" [Gertrude to Felix].

. . . "You seem to me very well placed, for enjoying. You have money and liberty and what is called in Europe 'a position.' But you take a painful view of life . . ."

. . . "To 'enjoy,' she began at last, "to take life—not painfully, must one do something wrong?" (73)

James's books deal again and again with the clash and struggle for dominance of values that he perceives as being inimical to one another, or as by definition ruling one another out. His international upbringing plus, I believe, his own particular proclivities made him acutely conscious that there was always another point of view on nearly anything. Certainly one result of his cosmopolitan experience was a skepticism about the ultimate validity of the mores of any culture. In 1872, in a letter quoted by Leon Edel, James wrote,

There comes a time when one set of customs, wherever it may be found, grows to seem to you about as provincial as another; and then I suppose it may be said of you that you have become a cosmopolite. You have formed the habit of comparing, of looking for points of difference and of resemblance, for present and absent advantages, for the virtues that go with certain defects, and the defects that go with certain virtues.[6]

His great dream—which is explicit in *The Ambassadors* —was of such a reconciliation or dialectical transcendence of these warring values that pleasure (aesthetic,

[6] *Henry James: The Conquest of London, 1870–1881* (New York, 1962), p. 33.

sensuous, sexual) might walk hand in hand with rectitude, the former unattended by corruption and the latter
by banality or Philistinism, but his books may be seen as
demonstrations of the failure of this dream.

The Europeans presents us with an initial dichotomy
between the goods and bads of Europe and America.
Each of the two characters involved in the happy ending
is seen, at first, in both negative and positive lights. Felix,
though he has a "charming nature" (17) and irrespres-
sibly "high spirits," (19) is "nothing but an obscure
Bohemian—a penniless correspondent of an illustrated
paper" (19) who dabbles in painting. Gertrude, though
virtuous and apparently somber (a New England merit),
is high-strung, moody, excitable: she is thought by her
father, sister, and the minister to be temperamentally
unreliable. "You have always needed advice" (166) is a
typical remark to her. Felix's nature is "intrinsically
joyous" (60), but that very fact, from his uncle's point of
view, is suspect: "He was not sure that Felix was
altogether safe. He was so bright and handsome and
talkative that it was impossible not to think well of him;
and yet it seemed as if there were something almost
impudent, almost vicious—or as if there ought to be—in a
young man being at once so joyous and positive"
(68).[7]

---

[7] While we do not share Mr. Wentworth's perspective—the
satire is self-evident—the whole book concerns itself with defining
the norm from which we are to evaluate the characters; this norm is
not clear until certain issues (such as who is going to marry whom)
are resolved. There is some uncertainty about how we are to take
Felix, for example, until near the end of the book, when there is a
quite explicit defense of him that puts to rest the slight doubt about
his reliability that the novel has maintained.

The Negative Imagination

One way in which James attempts to reconcile the polarities is to show that when all the facts are out, the negative sides of one set (a "set" includes one person from America, one from Europe) of protagonists are illusory. If the positive aspect of the European character is taste, plus a graceful capacity for pleasure and zest for life, its obverse is amorality, unscrupulousness. But when Felix finally reveals himself, we find he is an adventurer and immoralist *manqué*, even at bottom a "terrible Philistine," by which he means a "plain God-fearing man" (95). Later, conceding that he is "frivolous and penniless and shabby," he adds, "I have been a Bohemian—yes; but in Bohemia I always passed for a gentleman. . . . It was the liberty I liked, but not the opportunities! My sins were all peccadilloes; I always respected my neighbour's property—my neighbour's wife. . . . And then, *c'est fini!* It's all over. *Je ne range*" (164).

Similarly, if the positive aspect of the American character is virtue, the negative aspect of it is not merely suspicion of pleasure but an incapacity for it.[8] But Gertrude, under her somberness, is shown to be "very capable of enjoying, if the chance were given" (74) her, and the book attempts (with only partial success, as we shall see) to establish that her restlessness—part of what her father calls her "difficult temperament"—is symptomatic of nothing but thwarted spontaneity and good spirits, a sign of society's ills and not her own.

---

[8] Mr. Brand says, " 'You know it makes them [her father and sister] happy to think you will listen to me.'

"She gave a little laugh. 'It doesn't make them happy,' she said. 'Nothing makes them happy. No one is happy here' " (78).

The point of view about morality implicit in the novel is one identified with neither the America nor the Europe of their major representatives—Elder Wentworth on the one hand, the Baroness Münster on the other. These two worlds of course judge each other: "The Baroness . . . instantly felt that she had been observed to be fibbing. She had struck a false note. But who were these people to whom such fibbing [a polite flattery] was not pleasing?" (92). But both in turn are judged from the vantage point of some larger perspective, represented ultimately by Felix and Gertrude, whose union seems to bring together the best (gaiety and goodness) of both worlds and to leave out the worst. The latter is reinforced by the defeat of the set of protagonists in whom the negative sides are *real*. Both Mr. Wentworth and the Baroness lose; his stiffness is put down, her unscrupulousness.

The "solution" to the initial dichotomy is thus that the "bad" parts of both Europe and America are thwarted, the "good" parts triumph. But what does not emerge is a dialectic giving us a union in which the bads of either polarity are subsumed by and transcended in a new principle. For example, a marriage might have taken place between the Baroness and Acton (himself posited as a rather improbable combination of the "positive" traits of both civilizations: he is rich, celibate, and close to being a man of the world) if her fibbing had been relegated to the status of a venial sin or even possibly a moral act, under some system in which "truth" is not automatically the highest good, but perhaps charity or amiability or the sparing of someone's feelings. Or even the Baroness's fortune-hunting could have been put down without the total sacrifice of her possible union with an American: she could have fallen in love in spite of herself—with either a poor *or* a rich man.

So that even in this novel, which represents for James an unusual triumph of positive values, it was achieved without a genuine synthesis. The dichotomy in fact has been dissolved rather than resolved: the terms—"Bohemian" and "Philistine"—that were used to establish, characterize, and define the original conflict have become so nearly synonymous by the end of the novel that their sanctity as concepts (and in this case as moral opposites) has been compromised.

The equation of the two terms, of course, has been accomplished by the sophistry of Felix's distinction between enjoying the freedom to do but not the doing of some particular act, adultery or whatever. Nevertheless, the distinction, however unpersuasive, enhances the corrosion of the term's negative connotations, since it suggests the bohemian milieu can be "enjoyable" and benign (so long as one does not *do* anything). One result of this suggestion is that the automatic valuation of "Bohemianism" as something immoral has broken down to some extent. There is an ambience now attached to the word that is vaguely pleasant; its moral threat has been diminished.

But what has not occurred is a real ethical re-evaluation (of the kind Strether is ultimately to make of the relationship between virtue and sexuality in *The Ambassadors*) of the moral phenomena the term is meant to summarize, a synthesis in which the term might retain its original denotation (acting with disregard for conventional morality) but come to be seen as something

positive, or partly so, instead of negative: Felix's refusal to
act according to this value system still condemns it.
Moreover, by the end of the novel, Felix completely
capitulates; he isn't even going to hang round in his old
milieu any more (*"Je ne range"*). Still, an undermining of
some of the presuppositions of the term has taken
place.

A similar effort—ultimately abortive but nonetheless
one that weakens the hold of certain rigid presuppositions
—takes place in the novel with respect to Gertrude and
her "temperament." Conceding that it is difficult,[9] she
throws the blame for that fact right back at her accusers:
"Why do you call it difficult? [to her father] It might have
been easy, if you had allowed it. *You wouldn't let me be
natural.* I don't know what you wanted to make of me.
Mr. Brand was the worst" (166; italics mine). She is
never at any time guilty of *misdeeds*; that is not even in
question. The issue revolves entirely around her disposi-
tion; she is reproved for feeling "restless," "excited," or
"passionate." Spontaneity from their point of view is
somehow dangerous or threatening, something to be
curbed. Tacit in this notion is the assumption that basic
human "nature" is corrupt; man is the fallen animal, and
any feelings that have their origin in his nature (as
opposed to those springing from his moral education) are
perforce an index of that fact and thus suspect. And since

[9] Mr. Wentworth insists upon this characterization throughout
the book. Here is a typical passage that occurs near the end when
he is distraught at the suggestion that Gertrude marry her
Bohemian cousin: " 'Where are our moral grounds?' demanded Mr.
Wentworth, who had always thought Mr. Brand [the minister]
would be just the thing for a younger daughter with a peculiar
temperament" (168).

man the fallen animal is man with guilty knowledge of his own sexuality, an equation is established between being "natural" and being "sexual" (which is to say "immoral"). Gertrude's protest contains the seeds of another view, of course: maybe human beings have a right to be what they are and maybe what that is, is not in fact corrupt.

In the novel's effort to exonerate Gertrude, the hypocrisy of the first attitude is exposed. "I have been pretending all my life [Gertrude tells her father]; I have been dishonest; it is you that have made me so! . . . Why shouldn't I be frivolous, if I want? One has a right to be frivolous if it's one's nature." But the exoneration is incomplete. She continues, "No, I don't care for the great questions. I care for pleasure—for amusement. Perhaps I am fond of wicked things; it is very possible!" (110). In other words, she can be either "dishonest" and "good" or "honest" and "wicked" (that is, "frivolous").

Two value systems are clashing here, one based upon fidelity to and acceptance of one's "nature" (with an imperfect gesture in the direction of perceiving the latter as something positive), the other upon a rejection of that nature as fallen and an equation of "pleasure" with wickedness. The book is attempting, once again, to work toward some redefinition of, or new equation for, human existence in which feeling and morality do not exclude each other, and what this ultimately amounts to is a search for a concept of innocent (prefallen) sexuality. Though the effort is abortive, the process James is engaged in was a radical one in two senses: first, the equation he was struggling to arrive at was essentially liberal and modern while the one he was trying to overthrow was typically Victorian; second, the very juxtaposition of these two value systems creates a dialogue, and dialogue on sexual matters (i.e., in the sexual-moral nexus) was *not* characteristic of his time. *Monologues,* however, were. In fact, if Steven Marcus's analysis in *The Other Victorians: A Study of Sexuality and Pornography in Mid-Nineteenth-Century England* is sound at least in its general observations, we may say that there existed the pornographic monologue on the one hand—underground, occult, unacknowledged—and the medical-moral one on the other hand ("I should say that the majority of women [happily for them] are not very much troubled with sexual feeling of any kind" etc.[10]) —public, institutionalized, "official." Otherwise—publicly —silence,[11] except for contradictions *not recognized as such,* existing side by side, as Marcus points out, but in no relation to each other except their unperceived relation as logical opposites,[12] hence also in effect monologues (one of which, in this case, is unconsciously pornographic).

[10] (New York, 1966), p. 31. (Quoted from the surgeon William Acton.)

[11] The "characteristic Victorian arrangement," Marcus writes, was one "in which the existence of a whole universe of sexuality and sexual activity was tacitly acknowledged and actively participated in, while at the same time one's consciousness of all this was, as far as possible, kept apart from one's larger, more general, and public consciousness of both self and society" (163).

[12] "On the one hand, children are spoken of as pure and innocent and sexually quiescent; on the other, they are described as constantly threatened by horrid temptations, open to stimulation and corruption, and in danger of becoming little monsters of appetite. There is nothing to mediate between these two extreme states, no middle ground or connection between them. And the contradiction that children are both at once remains altogether unconscious." *Ibid.,* p. 15.

The Negative Imagination

There were other unrecognized ambiguities pertaining to sexuality that Marcus does not mention: the interpretations given mild hysterical manifestations (fainting, palpitations, tears, guilt, agitation,[13] restlessness, insomnia) in women, for example. Depending to some extent—but not entirely by any means—on their range of severity, such manifestations were understood alternatively as signs simply of delicate feminine nature;[14] of reaction to an unjust society;[15] of incipient or actual insanity, given equivocating medical names as Alice's illness was—"spinal neurosis," "nervous hyperaesthesia";[16] of some *moral* equivalent [17] thereof, the judgments of

[13] Alice James, speaking of the never-ending fight between her will and her impulses, recalls trying to study as a girl at school, "instead of shirking or wiggling thro' the most impossible sensations of upheaval." *The Diary of Alice James*, ed. Leon Edel (New York, 1964), p. 149.

[14] Alice James writes contemptuously of a Miss Leppington who visited her in England: "She is as delicate and spiritual-minded as if she had bloomed upon our rock-bound puritan coast. She clings so to a 'sense of sin,' for it's not automatic simply, as is usual, but from conviction that *she* worships a God who made her thus!—she apparently likes it." *Ibid.*, p. 45.

[15] She says of her closest friend and companion, Katharine Peabody Loring, who was *not* an invalid, that she stood for a "life lifted out of all material care or temptation to which all the rudimentary impulses were unknown, a collection simply of fantastic *un*productive emotions enclosed within tissue paper. Walls, rent equally by pleasure as by pain—animated by a never-ceasing belief in and longing for *action*, relentlessly denied, all safety-valves shut down in the way of 'the busy ineffectiveness of women.'" *Ibid.*, p. 151.

[16] *Ibid.*, p. 8.

[17] "If we wanted to analyze the profound structures of objectivity in the knowledge and practice of nineteenth-century psychiatry from Pinel to Freud, we should have to show in fact that such objectivity was from the start a reification of a magical nature, which could only be accomplished with the complicity of the

14

which might be clouded by the more neutral language of eccentricity (as in the case of Gertrude)—a nature given to "peculiarities," one that must be watched and that is an object of extreme concern—in other words the sign of something dangerously unpredictable, whose latent forces seem prone to spill over the bounds of propriety and ultimately reveal their own sexuality.

In each of the cases we have been discussing—the colliding moral constructs in *The Europeans;* the Victorian pornography that was the unacknowledged obverse of the "official" stance toward sexuality; and the shifting, alternative categories to which certain symptoms were unconsciously and more or less indiscriminately relegated —we are dealing with conflicting assumptions (fallen or guiltless, free or determined, and so forth) about or models for human nature. In this sense James, in dealing in ambiguities, was not unique. But he did two things that were unusual for his time: first, instead of trying to deny man's sexual nature, he accepted it as given, thereby breaking the "silence" maintained by the official ideology about at least certain aspects of sexuality,[18] thus admit-

---

patient himself, and beginning from a transparent and clear moral practice [of making the patient internalize the accusation and judgment of society upon his madness], gradually forgotten as positivism imposed its myths of scientific objectivity. . . . What we call psychiatric practice is a certain moral tactic contemporary with the end of the eighteenth century, preserved in the rites of asylum life, and overlaid by the myths of positivism." Michel Foucault, *Madness and Civilization: A History of Insanity in the Age of Reason,* tr. Richard Howard (New York, 1965), p. 276.

[18] Euphemistically, however: James always deals with sexual matters by some kind of indirection, articulating in disguised form what the Victorians (except for their pornography) generally did not articulate at all.

ting them into the public awareness. Second, instead of maintaining contradictions that were not recognized as such, he not only recognized but also deliberately brought them into juxtaposition, thus making their relation as contradictions a conscious, public fact. Both of these operations may in fact be regarded precisely as acts of consciousness and, for the period, radical ones indeed.

What James could not do, however—as we saw in the case of both Felix and Gertrude—was to synthesize the conflicting premises that were so characteristic of the structures of his imagination: his "dialogues" reached no conclusion. Nevertheless, to the extent that he made explicit and brought into conjunction widely opposed ways of seeing and understanding the universe, he was helping both to undermine some of the more rigid presuppositions of his age and to bring into existence a profoundly modern sensibility. Even when he utilized the categories of the official rhetoric (good and evil, chastity, and so forth), for instance, he did so in the service of foreign gods, either to upend the categories themselves or to bring them into continuous ironic contrast with vastly different assumptions about and modes simply of viewing, let alone understanding, human life.

In other ways, too, he was (in the English novel) an innovator: his books, for example, take for granted things like the fact that people, whether married or not, have lovers (as opposed or in addition to "falling in love"); or that children are attentive to and fascinated by sex.

Sexual betrayal of one kind or another is in fact one of his commonest themes. Moreover, he was interested not just in "normal" sexuality but in its various extremes: homosexuality, cradle-robbing, partner-switching, narcissism, voyeurism. In the period of the problem novels like *The Awkward Age, The Sacred Fount,* and *What Maisie Knew* the violation of innocence, Edmund Wilson points out, was a favorite theme of James, "with the victim in every case . . . a young or a little girl. . . . The real effectiveness of all these stories derives, not from the conventional pathos of a victim with whom we sympathize but from the excitement of the violation." [19]

He was lured too by diabolic and destructive fringes of experience for their own sakes—what Maggie in *The Golden Bowl* called "that fascination of the monstrous that temptation of the horribly possible" [20] and Rowland Mallet, in *Roderick Hudson,* the "gulf" of "destruction, annihilation, death." [21] In each case these are "good" characters visited by a gratuitous but overpowering impulse to ruin the people closest to them—as in fact they end up doing, inadvertently and not at the moment of their conscious temptation, though that moment may be regarded in each case as paradigmatic of the actual outcome of events.

But though he was drawn to certain extremities of experience and consciousness, he always was to encounter this sort of experience indirectly: by suggestion, innuendo, inference—all of the ways the characters communicate or

[19] "The Ambiguity of Henry James," in *A Casebook on Henry James's "The Turn of the Screw,"* ed. Gerald Willen (New York, 1960), p. 149. The text used is that of the 1948 revised and enlarged edition of Wilson's *The Triple Thinkers* (New York, 1948), pp. 82–132. The *Casebook* also uses, by permission of the author, a postscript dated 1959.

[20] New York ed. (New York, 1909), XXIV, 233. Citations from *The Golden Bowl* in my text are to this edition.

[21] New York ed. (New York, 1907), I, 314.

divine one another's meaning without words (his vision of her vision of his vision, and so forth) or in spite of words, since what is expressed by them usually means something other than it professes to. The bald facts are seldom stated openly.

The result of such an approach to such subject matter was that James offended the orthodox taste of both his own period (which was repressive anyway:*What Maisie Knew* was published in 1897, a year after *Jude the Obscure* caused its violent critical storm) and ours: the former because he assumed people, including children, have destructive impulses and sexual proclivities of every sort; the latter because he wasn't direct about rendering them. So a critic (quoted by James in the Preface to *What Maisie Knew*) wrote in his time that it was "disgusting" (just as Hardy was accused of going "out of his way to write of nastiness") for him to "attribute to [the child] Maisie so intimate an 'acquaintance' with the gross immoralities [her parents' various affairs, and in turn the affairs of their lovers] surrounding her"; [22] and another in ours said that James's heroes "seem never to exist except in the functioning of their intellects, they are only winged busts; all the weight of the flesh is absent. . . ." [23] Again, Edmund Wilson, writing of this period of James's development says, "There are plenty of love affairs now and plenty of irregular relationships [the absence of which Wilson had been bemoaning in James's earlier work], but there are always thick screens between them

[22] *The Art of the Novel*, p. 149.
[23] André Gide, "Henry James," *The Question of Henry James: A Collection of Critical Essays*, ed. F. W. Dupee (New York, 1945), p. 251.

and us; illicit appetites, maleficent passions, now provide the chief interest, but they are invariably seen from a distance." [24] And why not? Such remarks are based upon the simplest notions about art's obligation first to be "realistic" (i.e. in this case, to describe bed scenes—"you cannot enchant an audience with stories about men wooing women in which the parties either never get together or are never seen functioning as lovers" [25]) and second to engage and directly involve the spectator ("enchant" him). But James, though he certainly hoped to "interest" the reader, and intensely so, wasn't seeking to transport him through the naturalistic portrayal of strong passion, or the depiction of "real" three-dimensional persons in their ordinary activities. It is true that James insisted that the "moral sense" of a work of art depended upon the amount of "felt life" involved in producing it. What James meant by "life," however, was neither teeming throngs in their daily round nor the spontaneous overflow of powerful feeling, but rather a response of consciousness, "a mark made on the intelligence."

And in fact the "screens" in James are part of the fiber of his art: he explicitly sought "distance"—concerned as he was not with events in themselves but rather with the impact they made upon a fine observing intelligence. What he wished to depict was a consciousness in the process of mediating, interpreting, and reacting to certain critical appearances in the external world. He writes of a description of Isabel Archer, "It is a representation simply of her motionlessly *seeing*, and an attempt withal to make the mere still lucidity of her act as interesting as the

---

[24] *A Casebook*, p. 134.   [25] *Ibid.*, p. 132.

surprise of a caravan or the identification of a pirate." [26]

One might add that to make such a representation interesting, the reality seen must perforce be dense, obscure, not easily fathomable. The movement in James's works consists again and again of a character penetrating the obscurity, gradually or all at once; the "events" in James's novels are perceptions.[27]

In James's work typically there are several levels of communication by inference and indirection. In *What Maisie Knew,* for example, all communication is indirect; the people in this world seldom mean what they say, and when they do they believe they can say it with impunity since they cannot be understood by the child. They are wrong, because either at the time or retrospectively she makes the correct inference. The principle of the book is the depiction of her mind divining and reacting to the truth: its access to her consciouness and the response of the latter to it. In either of these two stances taken by the people of her world, there is a discrepancy between the overt statement and the intended communication, and that discrepancy has to do with the speaker's evaluation of the person spoken to—as either perspicacious (and hence able to grasp the real meaning of an intentionally ambiguous communication) or not (and hence not able to comprehend a clear statement).

Such depiction of the process of perception is quite different from the imitation of the free play of the mind in

---

[26] *The Art of the Novel,* p. 57.

[27] In this sense, what matters is not what two people do in bed, but rather the *fact* that they are lovers and that this fact has been hidden.

its random associations. Consciousness is James's field, but it is always consciousness focused, attentive, concentrated to the exclusion of all else upon the significance of particular signs and events in the present (as opposed to the past, though the present, once correctly understood, may bring to light a whole hidden past and enforce a wholly new understanding of previous appearances or cause a *known* past to be re-evaluated)—never consciousness "streaming." This process is essentially different from the Proustian "recovery of lost [as opposed to 'hidden'] realities in remembrance, a recovery released by some externally insignificant and apparently accidental occurrence."[28] The external event is *never* insignificant in James, indeed by definition is some pattern or occurrence that *has* significance (to the observing consciousness). Ones that do not are simply not depicted by him.

The particular aesthetic effects James sought—intensity, interest, scenic vividness, ironic contrast, and so forth—are related to this process of the imitation of an acutely focused mind observing and deciphering the meaning of significant but misleading appearances. Contrast and irony are achieved through the discrepancy between appearances and what lies behind them; something becomes interesting not because it necessarily is in itself, but because it is so *to* someone. In the Preface to *What Maisie Knew* James even congratulates himself for his success, through the medium of Maisie's consciousness, in transforming "appearances in themselves vulgar

[28] Erich Auerbach, *Mimesis: The Representation of Reality in Western Literature,* trans. Willard Trask (New York, 1957), p. 478.

and empty enough. They become, as she deals with them, the stuff of poetry and tragedy and art." [29]

Though I would sharply qualify that word "tragic," this novel is illuminating with respect to a number of these matters we have been discussing. For one thing, it is explicitly about the process of perception, of "knowing" in the sense of becoming aware, in spite of appearances suggesting the contrary, that something (or other) is the case. For another, it is an excellent example of James's utilization of moral rhetoric for purposes that challenge the validity of the normative attitudes implied by the very use of that vocabulary. Third, the novel's terrain is that area of ambiguity in human life and in its modes of comprehending itself which is due to the continuous collision of fictions about it. The system of ordering and hence investing reality with meaning involved in traditional concepts of "good" and "evil," man's freedom and yet his paradoxically fallen nature, his primary duty of obedience to a morally exacting if unpredictable creator and later to a compassionate but even more exacting redeemer, is one such fiction. But it is only one, as James knew very well, and though it has been a major one in Western civilization, its credibility as a structure was rapidly dwindling in his era. *What Maisie Knew* [30]

[29] *The Art of the Novel*, p. 147.

[30] New York ed. (New York, 1908), XI. Subsequent citations are to this edition. For those unfamiliar with this novel, Maisie, who is six at the book's start, is the child of divorced parents between whom she divides her time. Each of them uses her to carry (unwittingly) messages of vituperation to the other and each welcomes her because he thinks he is depriving the other of her company. She soon sees what she is being used for and plays dumb, consequently becoming less welcome. Both parents take lovers

opposes this fiction to others that tend by their very nature to call its presuppositions into quesion. Though he endows Maisie with virtue (as well as "no end" of sensibility) and considers that in her milieu she draws "some stray fragrance of an ideal across the scent of selfishness . . . sowing on barren strands, through the mere fact of presence, the seed of the moral life," [31] the effect that he sees resulting from this confrontation of virtue and selfishness is primarily a *dramatic* one, involving contrast, opposition, and reversal of expectations. What her innocence achieves, he says proudly, is to make "confusion worse confounded."

What James sought in this novel, the "red dramatic spark that glowed at the core of [his] vision," was what he called "the *full* ironic truth," [32] the truth that "with the best faith in the world . . . the child [would become] a centre and pretext for a fresh system of misbehavior."

No themes are so human [he continues] as those that reflect for us, out of the confusion of life, the close connexion of bliss and bale, of the things that help with the things that hurt, so dangling before us for ever that bright hard medal, of so

---

whom they wed. Maisie becomes the unintentional agent of her two stepparents meeting and subsequently becoming lovers. Each original parent also takes a new lover and, in the meantime, dumps Maisie. Her original governess, Mrs. Wix, tries to save Maisie from overexposure to the immoral influences surrounding her, but both Maisie and Mrs. Wix fall in love with Maisie's stepfather, Sir Claude. In the end, Maisie tries unsuccessfully to get him to go off with her alone and leave his lover (her stepmother) as she would leave Mrs. Wix, but he won't. She goes off with Mrs. Wix. Maisie "knows" or finds out about everyone's affairs with everyone in the course of the novel, as well as people's motives, duplicity, and so forth.

[31] *The Art of the Novel*, p. 143.   [32] *Ibid.*, p. 142.

strange an alloy, one face of which is somebody's right and ease and the other somebody's pain and wrong.[33]

But in spite of this "human" justification, the real fascination here is with the idea of disorder, especially centered around and caused by a child, and one who intends no ill. Her innocence is in fact called into the service not of a moral vision but of an ironic one: we are meant to *enjoy* (be interested in) the clash between the expectations set up by traditional views of the fate of goodness (to be, and be rewarded for being, the author of more good) and what actually happens to it here (becoming the author of ill). We could *not* enjoy it, of course, if we were not fully aware of the valuation traditional morality would put on Maisie's situation.

Moreover, her innocence itself is ambiguous—open to question, and very much a matter of definition. In the "theological" sense of the absence of knowledge of good and evil, she remains innocent throughout, since, though she always has knowledge and is acquiring more, it is knowledge unaccompanied by (ethical) judgment.[34] In effect, technical innocence becomes amorality. As a result of Maisie's seeming to know "without . . . seeming to condemn" (283), Mrs. Wix accuses her of lacking a moral sense. When Maisie is abandoned by her real parents, she wants her two stepparents (who she knows

[33] *Ibid.*, p. 143.

[34] Though she makes certain kinds of judgments—about people's looks, say, or their kindness or even their selfishness—she makes them without applying any *moral* category to them. Thus, she "knows" that her father or mother, or whoever, is selfish and dishonest and conducting an adulterous affair, but she does not judge these phenomena as "bad"—the concept and the affect that conventionally would attend it simply are not at her service.

24

are having an affair) to live with her and Mrs. Wix. The latter says that would be to condone their "crime," their "immorality." The child replies, "Why is it immorality?"

That question (whose relation to official Victorian ideology speaks for itself) is just one example in the book of a situation being exposed to the possibility of radically differing interpretations; here, as in many of James's novels, what is problematic [35] is not what is going on, but how we are to take it and which category, moral or otherwise, to which it belongs.

We are also meant to enjoy the repeated exposure or, as Edmund Wilson says, violation of her innocence. James defended this exposure (which his unnamed critic called "disgusting") on the ground that what gives Maisie "distinction . . . vitality and variety" is precisely that she preserves her identity even though the "tax" upon it is "monstrous." [36] Maisie's identity is preserved in the sense that she neither collapses under the weight of the pressures put on her nor becomes what the people around her want her to become: she resists them all, finally, including Mrs. Wix, who wants her to develop a "moral sense." [37]

The matter of her holding out was important to James:

[35] In *The Sacred Fount* the ambiguity shifts to the actual events: appearances refuse to be fathomed.

[36] *The Art of the Novel*, p. 150.

[37] By pretending imbecility she defeats her parents' wish to use her as a vehicle of their mutual malice. But Sir Claude's failure at the end to make her abandon Mrs. Wix and go off with himself and Mrs. Beale is *not* due to a final access of piety on Maisie's part; it is because he in turn won't agree to abandon Mrs. Beale. It is not to be moral that Maisie wants in the end but to live alone with Sir Claude.

. . . *some* intensity, some continuity of resistance being naturally of the essence of the subject. Successfully to resist (to resist, that is, the strain of observation and the assault of experience) what would that be, on the part of so young a person, but to remain fresh, and still fresh, and to have even a freshness to communicate? . . . She wonders [about her friends, etc.], in other words, to the end, to the death—the death of her childhood.[38]

In part, imputing this "truth of resistance" to his heroine mattered to James because of his always intense concern with dramatic effects and the values he felt were to be found in the very fact of a character's opposition to forces threatening to overwhelm it. He eventually objected to his second novel, *Roderick Hudson* (1875), on the grounds that the hero did not fight back, fell apart too fast, and had too much of "the principle of collapse": " 'On the basis of so great a weakness,' one hears the reader say, 'where was your idea of the interest? On the basis of so great an interest, where is the provision for so much weakness?' " [39]

But in the remarks about Maisie just quoted, there is a strange admixture of elements, of contradictory impulses, language that communicates a delight in the dramatic potential of his subject and *seems* to with respect to the triumph of innocence but that, when examined in context, communicates something quite different and far more complex. What has Maisie to "wonder" about but the meaning of the behavior of the various adults who make up her universe?—behavior that the author characterizes in the Preface as "deplorable" and "monstrous," while praising the "vivacity of [her] intelligence" vibrating in

[38] *The Art of the Novel,* p. 146.   [39] *Ibid.,* p. 13.

"the infected air" and the little girl flourishing in her "immoral world." It is her "wonder" over this tainted environment, an environment "assaulting" her sensibility from the age of six with its sexuality, that is supposed to be the "freshness" that she has to communicate!

A universe in which innocence, while being exposed and assaulted, somehow miraculously survives the assault has familiar enough analogues: Maisie's plight, as well as her capacity to endure it, is reminiscent of the heroine-victims of pornographic novels—O, Anne (in Jean de Berg's *The Image*), and others, who bounce back restored and unfaltering after an evening of rape, mutilation, and scourging. The violation here is all symbolic of course, and communicated by innuendo. Nevertheless, the universe of this novel is a completely (and "perversely") sexualized one, provided one accepts James's definition of "experience" as "the impact of events upon an intelligence": in other words if one accepts his equation of experience with certain motions of consciousness.[40] One might call *What Maisie Knew* a latent pornographic novel.[41]

Moreover, the actual tone of the novel toward the "infected" characters and their whole sexual scene is quite

[40] An equation that he made again and again, and that had its origins in one of his earliest perceptions of himself absorbed from his elders when he was a small boy, to the effect that "the only form of riot or revel" he would ever know "would be that of the visiting mind." (*Autobiography: A Small Boy and Others; Notes of a Son and Brother; The Middle Years*, ed. F. W. Dupee (New York, 1956), p. 16.

[41] And as in pornography, there is a continual ironic interplay between the responses of conventional mores and the subterranean responses that it has traditionally been one function of the former to suppress.

different from that communicated by the kinds of terms James uses in the Preface, though, as we have seen, to relish the "full irony" we must be able to draw upon our experience of the normative attitudes such terms imply. But we can't rest with these attitudes or indeed with any: this book renders its material from a multiplicity of perspectives, and none is final. In that sense it may be said that the book is about the ambiguity of human meaning and value, or of meaning in the making and unmaking, since it presents to us various and contradictory modes of categorizing phenomena and does not adjudicate between them. Some of these modes are implicit, to be inferred by and imputed to the reader on the basis of (presumably) agreed-upon general experience; there are varying degrees of explicitness with the others.

To a certain extent, there is a division of viewpoints entailed in the very narrative mode of the novel. To begin with, Maisie's sensibility so transforms what comes into its ken that what would ordinarily be vulgar or banal is perceived by her as fabulous (like a fairy tale) and exotic.[42] But Maisie herself is not the narrator and it is the narrator's consciousness, as we shall see, that determines the book's tone, insofar as there is an "official" one.[43] The *narrator's* attitude (though he comments

---

[42] A countess, one of her father's lovers, is described as "the short fat wheedling whiskered person" (194) in "her dazzling gilded drawing-room," which, when Maisie enters it, makes her feel as if "the Arabian Nights had quite closed round her." Everything in the room has the "pitch of the wondrous" (175).

[43] The whole concept of "tone" has to be rethought when it is applied to works that render multiple views, or to a work in which a view, though single, is, in Wayne Booth's term, "unreliable." In *The Rhetoric of Fiction* (Chicago, 1962), Booth insists it is the author's moral duty to make the moral stance of his work

directly very seldom and even then his comments may be at variance with other inferable stances he takes) toward the major characters and their sexual vagaries is worldly, amused, sophisticated, and totally unshocked: quite a different stance from that suggested by the language in James's Preface.

James felt that his artistic challenge was to present everything ("the whole situation surrounding her") to the reader but to give it "only through the occasions and connexions of her [Maisie's] proximity and her attention; only as it might pass before her and appeal to her." Although he wished to restrict what was seen to what she saw, he felt that he couldn't use her language: "Small children have many more perceptions than they have terms to translate them; their vision is at any moment much richer . . . than their prompt, their at all producible, vocabulary." [44]

So that though the events of the novel are limited to what Maisie sees and reacts to, the actual narrator, while entirely sympathetic to Maisie, is an anonymous, disembodied, adult, ironic voice who speaks "in figures that are not yet at her command." [45] Maisie's "simpler conclusions," James writes, quite depend on her own terms, "but our own commentary constantly attends and amplifies." [46] The narrator—and the reader—are "not

---

unambiguous; he also insists all communication depends on the author's doing so. Such views are not only hard to defend but exclude almost all contemporary literature.

[44] *The Art of the Novel*, p. 145.   [45] *Ibid.*, p. 146.

[46] The phrase "our own" does not mean that James himself is the narrator. (For an excellent discussion of this distinction between author and narrator, see *The Rhetoric of Fiction*, pp. 67 ff. Booth calls the latter the "second self" or "implied author.") Here the nar-

more invited but only more expert critics" [47] of the events that befall her.

Maisie's less simple perceptions are put into the *narrator's* terms; he transposes—in James's word "translates"—her nonverbal awareness into verbal awareness, which is to say consciousness as we ordinarily think of it. In this sense it may be said that he *is* her consciousness. The result is a double displacement: the narrator has no "concern" of his own but takes hers;[48] Maisie has no (or none other than a simple) language of her own, but takes (is provided with) his. This displacement imposes a considerable distance between us and the heroine and is one of the things that account for a certain attenuated, detached, disembodied quality that the novel has.

Such duality built into the very mode of presentation of events is quite characteristic of James, and is sometimes elaborated to an extremely complex degree, as we shall see in *The Golden Bowl*. It is to be distinguished from the other forms of multiple perspective that we have been or will be discussing (opposed interpretations of the same events by characters without any one being given final authority in the novel; reliance upon standard or "com-

---

rator has various degrees of closeness to his subject. Sometimes he views her as an object outside himself: "It was to be the fate of this patient little girl to see much more than she at first understood, but also even at first to understand much more than any little girl" (9). But he also sees what she sees, and through her eyes; he is privy to her thoughts, or at least some of them, and passes on to us the movements of her perceptions—but in *his* words. Sometimes he merely records dialogue.

[47] *The Art of the Novel*, p. 145.

[48] "It is her relation [to "the facts of her spectacle"], her activity of spirit, that determines all our own concern" (*The Art of the Novel*, p. 146).

mon" attitudes in the reader to be juxtaposed ironically with others; the utilization of certain words in a manner that destroys their ordinary connotations if not denotations) in the sense that there is at least no divergence of aims or clash of sympathies between the narrator and the heroine. But it is akin to the above phenomena in that it involves a division or fragmentation of perspective. In this case, we experience the consciousness of the narrator as it is translating—making conscious—the perceptions of the central character, who is herself engaged almost exclusively in deciphering a mysterious, misleading reality in which there appears a discrepancy between what the other characters do or say and what they mean—that is, between their consciousnesses and some mask by which they obscure them.

These varied refractions of the material through the media of several consciousnesses (a process that always fascinated James) involves an engagement with the work that is complex and contemplative but not necessarily intense. If anything, such a technique detaches the reader from any strong emotional response. Indeed it almost precludes such response. What we become "interested in" is not so much the ultimate fate of Maisie—we are not indifferent to her, but it simply is not possible to feel torn apart by her plight[49]—as the complexities and ironies resulting from the presentation of the varied and clashing perspectives.

Apart from the narrative mode, there is complexity in the novel that results from discrepancies between two

[49] In fact, if anything—and this is in line with the pornographic features of the novel—the effect is titillating rather than horrific.

characters' views of the same event. At the end of the novel, for example, Mrs. Wix accuses Sir Claude of being responsible for Maisie's lost "moral sense":

"You've nipped it in the bud. [Because Maisie is in love with him and is eager to forsake Mrs. Wix to be with him.] You've killed it when it had begun to live."

She was a newer Mrs. Wix than ever, a Mrs. Wix high and great; but Sir Claude was not after all to be treated as a little boy with a missed lesson. "I've not killed anything," he said; "on the contrary I think I've produced life. I don't know what to call it—I have n't even known how decently to deal with it, to approach it; but, whatever it is, it' s the most beautiful thing I' ve ever met—it' s exquisite, it' s sacred." (354)

These radically opposed interpretations of the meaning of the same occurrences are left open; they are unresolved. Nothing *in the book* insists that one is right, or more nearly so, than the other. The best we can make is a kind of negative decision: since both characters are "interested" parties in one way or the other, we have to take that into account and allow for possible distortions. Mrs. Wix's tone may be "great" but she is in love with Sir Claude too.[50] Nor does the book support her sense of outrage over Maisie's amorality. But even when we make these allowances, there is no way to determine any final attitude to take toward Maisie.

The very positing of these two unadjudicated views, however, makes the reader encounter them as *possible*

---

[50] Moreover, she makes some strange distinctions that create a certain dubiousness about her own "moral sense": "While they [Maisie's father and one of his lovers] were about it at any rate, since they were ruining *you* [Maisie], they might have done it so as to spare an honest woman [herself]" (283).

ways of understanding and judging what has happened. But only possible ways: they never leave the realm of potentiality. They become hypothetical models. The fact that they are not resolved means there is always something open-ended about them: either *might* be valid. Conversely, either might *not* be valid. The technique thus both raises the possibility of and calls into question the validity of both points of view.

In his chapter on the unreliable narrator in *The Aspern Papers*, Wayne Booth makes a remark that we may take as a general complaint against James: "Again and again in the story one is forced to throw up his hands and decide that James simply has provided insufficient clues for the *judgments which he still quite clearly expects us to be able to make*" (italics mine).[51] Booth does not document that last—and crucial—assertion, or indicate what in the story suggests that "clear" expectation on the author's part.

This much I believe is true: in order to experience an ironical effect we must be able not so much to *make* a certain judgment as to contemplate its possibility—to test it out hypothetically and to understand the basis for a given character's making it, or at least professing to make it. So, for example, with respect to the clash between Mrs. Wix and Sir Claude, one has to comprehend or have some familiarity with the value system that would allow someone to pronounce as "sacred" what has happened to Maisie. That system is clearly one which gives allegiance to passion and personal commitment and which does *not* condemn sexuality—even in one so young. All those cluster of things—energy, love, "life forces," and so

[51] *The Rhetoric of Fiction*, p. 361.

on—are the "goods" implicit in Sir Claude's view. If one does not understand that (and some of James's early readers of the novel didn't), then the ironical experience resulting from the clash of this view with the one that equates sexuality and sexual exposure of the young with moral evil is lost. But this does not mean that the reader is necessarily expected to "make a judgment" himself, or even that it would be desirable for him to do so. Instead, in the context of *this* novel, he experiences the possibility first of this meaning, and then of that. Next he experiences the abolition of each possibility in a continuously subjective universe, one engaged in meaning-making but with no pretensions to objective truth: a universe engaged in the creation, juxtaposition, collision, and annihilation of fictions.

Some of the steps of this process are familiar to us today as *conscious* techniques of contemporary writers.[52] But they are not new: "The destruction of literary texts is not an invention of contemporary critics; from Flaubert to Beckett, almost every important modern writer has been engaged in the subversion of his own meanings, in a more or less violent refusal to believe in or be limited by the expressiveness of his language." [53]

With James what is problematical is not the use of the

[52] "What constitutes the novelist's strength is precisely that he invents, that he invents quite freely, without a model. The remarkable thing about modern fiction is that it asserts this characteristic quite deliberately, to such a degree that invention and imagination become, at the limit, the very subject of the book." (Alain Robbe-Grillet, *For a New Novel: Essays on Fiction*, trans. Richard Howard [New York, 1965], p. 32.)

[53] Leo Bersani, "From Bachelard to Barthes," *Partisan Review*, XXXIV (Spring 1967), 228.

technique but the degree to which he was conscious of it and deliberately exploited its possibilities. It is sometimes hard to tell, especially in extremely ambiguous works like *The Golden Bowl* and *The Turn of the Screw*.[54] In the case of *The Sacred Fount*, whose meaning has been much debated, it seems to me clear that he was conscious of exactly what he was doing, and that ambiguity and the possible meanings one can consign to appearance, the operations of the imagination upon selected data, are precisely what that book is *about*. And here again, to approach such a novel by asking the question "Who is right?" when it is pre-eminently clear that the evidence for making such a decision is simply not there, is to waste breath. We should start from what we are given, as James said: "We must grant the artist his subject, his idea, his *donnée:* our criticism is applied only to what he makes of it."[55]

What we are "given" in *The Sacred Fount* are two hypothetical models or constructs for "explaining" some observed facts—models that contradict each other. Later

[54] That work is a *tour de force* of the *double entendre:* provided one accepts the possibility of the governess's getting a description of Quint in town, every single event, remark, perception in it is susceptible of two radically opposed interpretations, as was remarked upon by Edmund Wilson in "The Ambiguity of Henry James." Wilson himself changed his mind three times between 1934 and 1959, and kept asking, "Which is the correct interpretation?" a question that is, I suggest, the wrong one altogether. It seems not to have occurred to commentators to take as its *donnée* the fact that the work sustains the double possibility, and proceed from there.

[55] "The Art of Fiction," *The Great Critics: An Anthology of Literary Criticism,* ed. James Harry Smith and Edd Winfield Parks, (New York, 1951), p. 662.

there becomes some question about the nature of the observed facts themselves; when the claim is made to the narrator by one of the principal characters that these are different than both had assumed, another model is built upon the "new" version of the facts, and is again contradicted. The universe we are in, once more, is a universe of meaning-making and unmaking, of the creation and abolition of fictions, for none of which any absolute claim is made, and *that is that*.[56] The only "necessity" imposed upon the constructs is that they account for the observed data—a necessity of internal consistency, a logic that the insane are gifted at. It is a universe of the arbitrary, one that bows only to the laws of persuasion; in that sense it is a rhetorical universe—the two principal characters are like embattled orators whose concern is not with uncovering the truth but with imposing their model of plausibility. That model triumphs which is the "wittiest" in the sense of possessing the most ingenuity and of blocking the most exits (logical outs) by which the foe might escape; the defeated narrator after his rival (Mrs. Brissenden) has finally put

---

[56] Booth mentions in passing but unfortunately fails to explore the implications of Ian Watt's suggestion that "the novel is essentially an ambiguous form; the rise of the novel is itself a reflection of 'the transition from the objective, social and public orientation of the classical world to the subjective, individualist and private orientation' of modern life and literature. As the novel sought what he calls 'realism of presentation,' in a world in which reality itself came to seem more and more ambiguous, relativistic, and mobile, it inevitably sacrificed something of the 'realism of assessment' of other genres." Booth acknowledges that "there is certainly something to this claim" but adds that "this does not mean, however, that novels should or must be ambiguous." *The Rhetoric of Fiction,* pp. 386–387.

him down with a "my poor dear, you *are* crazy, and I bid you good night!" has this last straw of consolation for himself: "I *should* certainly never again, on the spot, quite hang together, even though it wasn't really that I hadn't three times her method. What I too fatally lacked was her tone." [57]

Booth's prescription that a work is "morally" obliged to make its moral orderings clear is inadequate to deal with and precludes any appreciation of works like *The Sacred Fount* or *What Maisie Knew*. Furthermore, even when intended as in more traditional literature to "instruct," one basic function of such orderings and of "values" in general—public or private [58]—has always been aesthetic. They are one of many kinds of orderings in literary works, or structures providing some kind of coherency, as do in their way "plot"; repetition (or, to use William Burroughs' term, "mosaic") of sound, metaphor, or other figures; rhythm: all of which work to produce "patterns" of one kind or another. It may be the purpose of a given work—and this is especially true of certain contemporary works—to undercut its own patterns at least insofar as they suggest "significance," but patterns are nevertheless there.

Moral orderings may be used to establish or heighten the emotional effect of a work by classifying or categorizing people and their actions in order to arouse certain responses—dread, scorn, detachment, affection—both to

[57] (New York, 1953), p. 319.
[58] "Virginia Woolf . . . was haunted by the sense that older writers could depend upon an audience with public norms, while she must construct her values as she went, and then impose them, without seeming to do so, on the reader" (*The Rhetoric of Fiction*, p. 392).

and entailed in the category: say, "knaves," or "fools." When someone not essentially a fool behaves like one, or when a ruthless man goes after a "good" but too-trusting man, it occasions a sense of dread, impending peril, and so forth. The effectiveness of these or any such categories depends first upon the reader's *knowledge* of them and what they imply and second upon his hypothetical or imaginative (but not upon his real) concurrence in them for the duration of the play or story.

Some works, as we have indicated, demand an imaginary participation in a multiplicity of views at least some of which are contradictory, and the experiencing of the clash of possible meanings that might be attached to any one event, without asking or expecting us to take a stance one way or the other. Indeed it might be the assumption of a given work that no final stance is possible.

James often uses the language of traditional morality not to explore moral questions per se but as one way of structuring reality that is then brought into opposition with other very different ways, frequently to the destruction or cancellation of both or at least to the demonstration of their inability to support and gratify the "total" human being. The interest lies in the engagement and clash—and perhaps for James the failure—of the structures.

Unlike that of Virginia Woolf, who also rendered reality from a multiplicity of views, James's aim was not "synthesis" and hence the "design of a close approach to objective reality by means of numerous subjective impressions received by various individuals." [59] In fact, one of

[59] *Mimesis*, p. 473.

the characteristics of James's sensibility is precisely the *inability* to engage in a real dialectical process or to reconcile conflicting if partial points of view. He is forever *dividing* reality into sets of mutually exclusive possibilities—possibilities each of which furthermore is attended by a negative consequence. Such synthesis as James was able to achieve was purely formal, a function of the design or structure of his novels, and it is to some of the consequences of this fact that we now turn our attention.

James is still a key figure in an argument, which he himself helped to initiate, about the nature and function of fiction and its relation to life. The argument is based upon the assumption that "reality" is contingent, shapeless, various, "sloppy," inexplicable, capricious—in this all the parties agree, though, as we shall see in a moment, James dealt with certain problems for the "painter of life" implicit in such a notion by insisting on two different meanings of the term "life" and by adopting when necessary a definition that enabled him (he thought) to take his place in the mimetic tradition. The disagreement itself has concerned the relations of this contingent reality to art, with one side insisting that art faithfully imitate, the other that it abrogate, that reality.

In the first stand we get the preoccupation with verisimilitude that with the exception of the symbolist movement was generally typical of nineteenth-century art [60] and that persists to this day—the more or less complete, externalized, and naturalistic description of

[60] Exceptions will come readily to mind: Dickens was in many ways a surrealist; Mrs. Gaskell in her novels; the Brontës.

"real" persons and their ordinary physical, temporal, and social milieu. Thus, in an article he wrote in 1915, H. G. Wells attacks James's formal concerns, accusing him of seeking a specious unity in his works, whereas

if the novel is to follow life it must be various and discursive. Life is diversity and entertainment, not completeness and satisfaction. All actions are half-hearted, shot delightfully with wandering thoughts—about something else. All true stories are a felt of irrelevances. But James sets out to make his novels with the presupposition that they can be made continuously relevant.[61]

Similarly, Edith Wharton wrote in 1934,

I was naturally much interested in James's technical theories and experiments, though I thought, and still think, that he tended to sacrifice to them that spontaneity which is the life of fiction. Everything, in the latest novels, had to be fitted into a predestined design.[62]

This stance continues, with certain elaborations, to this day. In 1959, in her article "The Sublime and the Beautiful Revisited," Iris Murdoch wrote,

Reality is not a given whole. An understanding of this, a respect for the contingent, is essential to imagination, as opposed to fantasy. Our sense of form, which is an aspect of our desire for consolation, can be a danger to our sense of reality as a rich receding background. Against the consolations of form, the clean crystalline work, the simplified fantasy myth, we must pit the destructive power of the now so

---

[61] "Of Art, of Literature, of Mr. Henry James," *The Modern Tradition: Backgrounds of Modern Literature*, ed. Richard Ellmann and Charles Feidelson, Jr. (New York, 1965), p. 326.

[62] *A Backward Glance* (New York, 1934), p. 190.

unfashionable naturalistic idea of character. Real people are destructive of myth, contingency is destructive of fantasy and opens a way for the imagination.[63]

In the second stand we get the more abstract preoccupation with the creation of an aesthetic artifact that began in the 1850's and is generally typical of twentieth-century art—an emphasis on patterns, structures (of whatever kind), forms, and the properties of forms such as balance, antithesis, repetition, contrast. Such preoccupation leads finally to the notion that invention—the operations of the imagination and the arbitrary creation of forms—is itself the subject of art, a notion that is antimimetic in that it constitutes a rejection of the "lifelike" or the "natural" in favor of creation, as Robbe-Grillet says, "without a model." [64]

This distinction between approaches to art has to be understood as one of degree, not kind. It may be true, as Ortega y Gasset insists, that perception "of 'lived' reality and perception of artistic form . . . are essentially incompatible because they call for a different adjustment of our perceptive apparatus," [65] but *all* perception

[63] *The Yale Review*, December 1959, 241–271. See also John Goode, "Character and Henry James," *New Left Review*, No. 40 (November–December 1966), 55–75. Goode quotes Murdoch and suggests that in the novels after 1896, James sacrificed "the autonomy of self to the autonomy of form."

[64] *For a New Novel*, p. 32.

[65] *The Dehumanization of Art and Other Writings on Art and Culture* (New York, 1956), p. 23. He explains the difference in "adjustment" by an analogy of the eye focusing on the windowpane, hence blurring the reality beyond it, or ignoring, forgetting the existence of the window and seeing only the three-dimensional real world outside. The latter is his image of the typical nineteenth-century activity in art, the former of twentieth-century activity.

involves the transformation and organization by the mind of data (sensory impulses) received from the world. Similarly, anyone's notion of what constitutes the "life-like" (or quotidian reality), let alone the imitation of it in art, itself involves selection, patterning, and the imposition of structure: for example, "x is (belongs to the category of the) real, y is unreal." The mediated experience of the external world, the making of forms which constitute both that experience and our knowledge of and responses to it, is the characteristically *human* activity.[66] And since this is the case, there is a "model" for the act of creation or form-making in the ordinary operations of the mind,[67] which may be said to mime itself when engaged in the conscious creation of an aesthetic artifact. *All* its activities are "creative" in this sense, and even madmen inhabit a world of forms.

The distinction of the approaches is nevertheless useful in categorizing different modes of form-making engaged in by the mind in its creative activity, in particular the degree to which these approximate the results (i.e. the specificity of ordinary perception) or the processes of its own activities.[68] It is perhaps, as Ortega suggests, a

[66] Along these lines, Leo Bersani criticizes Frank Kermode's notion that the relation of art to life is that of "fictive orders to real chaos." Bersani also criticizes Kermode for neglecting the implications of his own remark that the "'formlessness of reality may . . . be just another human way of imagining the inhuman.'" "Variations on a Paradigm," *New York Times Book Review*, June 11, 1967, pp. 6, 45.

[67] This is made vivid for some people with visual experiences under marijuana, in which, without actual hallucination, ordinary seeing becomes "painterly."

[68] These processes are what Ortega calls taking our "ideas for what they are—mere subjective patterns" but making them live,

matter of adjustment of focus, since in either mode the other is implicit: there are "patterns" (of selection, rhythm, whatever) in "realistic" novels, and there is texture, sensuousness, and particularity in even the most abstract of artifacts. Nevertheless, in a given work one mode will be predominant.

James himself falls into the formal mode, though he sought for a certain balance. He acknowledged and admired the "energy directly exhibited" (a quality not characteristic of his own art) of realists like Tolstoy, Wells, and Bennett and praised them for bringing into fiction a "saturation and possession" of the common human scene that had been absent for three or four generations. And he insisted that this capacity constituted "on behalf of the novelist, as on that of any painter of things seen, felt or imagined, just one-half of his authority." [69] But the other half of this authority lay in the *use* to which this capacity for rendering the denseness and particularity of life was put: there must, he wrote in 1914, be some controlling "centre of the interest," some "pointed intention," some "sense of the whole" [70] behind the selection of any and every detail. A picture "without composition," he writes,

slights its most precious chance for beauty. . . . There may in its absence be life, incontestably, as . . . Tolstoi's "Peace and War" [and "Les Trois Mousquetaires"] have it; but what do

---

" 'realizing' " them, so that "we give three-dimensional being to mere patterns, we objectify the subjective, we 'worldify' the immanent" (35).

[69] "The Younger Generation," *The Modern Tradition*, p. 318.

[70] *Ibid.*, p. 320.

such large loose baggy monsters, with their queer elements of the accidental and the arbitrary, artistically *mean?* . . . There is life and life, and as waste is only life sacrificed and thereby prevented from "counting," I delight in a deep-breathing economy and an organic form.[71]

"Life" in this second sense [72]—the sense that James insists his art renders—is thus diametrically opposed to that variety, abundance, energy, messiness, and contingency that characterize the image of reality held in common by all these writers we have mentioned—whatever their stance about art—as well as by later writers like Sartre and Camus. James too shares this fiction, in so far as it applies to *life:* "Really, universally, relations stop nowhere, and the exquisite problem of the artist is eternally but to draw, by a geometry of his own, the circle within which they shall happily *appear* to do so." [73] Or again, "No action [in fiction] . . . was ever made historically vivid without a certain *factitious compactness*" (italics mine).[74] In relation to art, he is quite insistent upon his rejection of the chance, the "loose," the unnecessary; any "development" the artist indulges in must not only be *"indispensable* to the interest" (italics his) but "rigorously so." [75]

James thus shares with a certain group of moderns—

---

[71] *The Art of the Novel,* p. 84.

[72] Which "counts" when it counts "to someone," makes a mark or impression on (if possible) a "finely registering mind." James's second definition of life really comes down to this: *a response of consciousness.* Hence his preference for rendering "somebody's impression" of the "affair at hand" rather than that affair itself.

[73] *The Art of the Novel,* p. 5.   [74] *Ibid.,* p. 15.
[75] *Ibid.,* p. 5.

Sartre, Gide, Camus, Genet, Robbe-Grillet, Burroughs —the notion that at least so far as its formal properties are concerned, art is in opposition to life, providing patterns of coherence (as the mosaic in *Naked Lunch*), shapes, structures (like the jazz tune in *Nausea*) with a beginning, middle, and end (even if, as in several of Genet's plays, like the famous serpent with its tail in its mouth, the ending is the beginning again) that are not to be found in life. (Hence, perhaps, James's irritation when, once he had picked up a "germ" for a story or novel from a piece of gossip briefly delineating a situation, his hostess would try to tell him the outcome and details of what "really" happened.[76])

What is extraordinary is the amount of vituperation that has been heaped on his head (including by Gide) for this attention to formal concerns and for what has seemed to a number of critics to be a consequent attenuation in the vitality (and moral worth) of his works.[77] There is, of course, a general tendency in English and American criticism to insist that fiction follow the tradition, laid down by Wells and others, of drawing from and depicting dense social reality[78] for the purpose of

[76] "He never wanted all the facts, which might stupefy him, but only enough to go on with, hardly enough to seem a fact at all." R. P. Blackmur, Introduction, *The Art of the Novel*, p. xv.

[77] See, for example, F. R. Leavis, *The Great Tradition* (Garden City, New York, 1954), p. 196, on *The Golden Bowl:* "It is as if his interest in his material had been too specialized, too much concentrated on certain limited kinds of possible development, and as if in the technical elaboration expressing this specialized interest he had lost his full sense of life and let his moral taste slip into abeyance."

[78] As Susan Sontag writes, "The critics' retrograde awareness of the impressive new claims staked out by modern literature, linked

offering "a help to conduct" or "a means of union among men joining them together in the same feelings, and indispensable for the life and progress toward well-being of individuals and of humanity." [79] But this tendency alone does not, I feel, sufficiently account for the general irritation with James for his concern with form, a concern that has become a commonplace of serious modern art.

A factor equally as important, I think, is the degree to which James is, but has been insufficiently recognized as being, a transitional figure straddling two historical periods and sharing some characteristics with each, often to the annoyance of readers from both periods. In some ways, he is the first "modern" novelist in English: in his awareness of, attention to, and deliberate experiment with modes of composition; in his use of the controlling "point of view" and the consequent objectification of patterns of consciousness as the major characteristic of his art; in his concern with aesthetic and formal ends; in his insistence upon the freedom of the artist to be granted and judged in terms of his *donnée* and to serve no other master than art itself; in his rendering of a multiplicity of viewpoints without positing some final objective truth; in his upending of traditional moral categories in the service of a demonic imagination; in his preoccupation with extreme

---

with their chagrin over what was usually designated as 'the rejection of reality' and 'the failure of the self' endemic in that literature, indicates the precise point at which most talented Anglo-American literary criticism leaves off considering structures of literature and transposes itself into the criticism of culture." "The Pornographic Imagination," *Partisan Review*, XXXIV (Spring 1967), 181–212.

[79] Leo Tolstoy, "What Is Art? and Other Essays," *The Modern Tradition*, pp. 300–309.

and perverse states of sensibility; and even, it could be argued, in the very qualities of tediousness, effeteness, ennui, monotony, and stylistic elaborateness that can make him so exasperating to read even while he is fascinating (sometimes the exasperation is one of the sources of the fascination).

But, as Harold Rosenberg remarks with respect to contemporary painting, innovation itself is not enough to constitute a School (or, in James's case, a whole new movement): "To form a School in modern times not only is a new painting consciousness needed but a consciousness of that consciousness—and even an insistence upon certain formulas." [80]

And finally it is precisely his lack of a conscious avant-garde attitude that, in spite of the remarkable Prefaces, keeps us from regarding James as a direct founder of modernism. He of course bore enormous direct *influence* on writers like Edith Wharton and Conrad,[81] who in turn as a writer was, along with Hardy, the recipient of Virginia Woolf's "unconditional gratitude" (whereas she merely "thanks" Wells, Bennett, and Galsworthy).[82] Gide

---

[80] *The Tradition of the New* (New York, 1961), p. 24. Rosenberg's phrase could itself almost serve as a formula for contemporary thought, which characteristically analyzes its own methodology and lays bare its own assumptions instead of taking them as givens not to be questioned or even recognized.

[81] F. W. Dupee records a fragment of a letter from Conrad to James, written after Conrad had finished reading *The American*: "I sat for a long while with the closed volume in my hand going over the preface in my mind and thinking—that is how it began, that's how it was done." *Henry James: His Life and Writings* (New York, 1956), p. 244.

[82] *The Common Reader: First Series* (New York, 1953), p. 151.

wrote about James, and was to have met him in 1915 in England (though he abandoned the trip at the last moment); he had a long talk about him with Charles du Bos in Paris in 1920 and more than once used James's title "the figure in the carpet" as an image for someone he was discussing.[83] Joyce refers to James in passing in a review of another novelist.[84] Claims have been made for his influence even on Hemingway.[85]

But in spite of his acquaintance with French literature, James was hostile to that revolutionary movement, symbolism (many of whose concerns he profoundly shared), which began with the publication of Baudelaire's translations of Poe's tales in 1852 and which marked the conscious shift into the modern literary sensibility. He never wrote an essay on Poe—a conspicuous gap in his writings on American letters, as Leon Edel points out in the Introduction to *The American Essays of Henry James*—and his essay on Baudelaire, first published in 1878, was supercilious and unappreciative.[86] Of Edmond

[83] *The Journals of André Gide: 1889–1949*, trans. Justin O'Brien (New York, 1956), I (1889–1924), pp. 206, 298. Also II (1924–1949), pp. 23, 94.

[84] *The Critical Writings of James Joyce*, ed. Ellsworth Mason and Richard Ellmann (New York, 1959), p. 118.

[85] Austin Warren, *Rage for Order: Essays in Criticism* (Ann Arbor, Michigan, 1959), p. 120.

[86] " 'Le Mal?' we exclaim: you do yourself too much honour. This is not Evil; it is not the wrong; it is simply the nasty!' " and so forth. On Poe, he writes that with "all due respect" to his "very Original genius," to "take him with more than a certain degree of seriousness is to lack seriousness oneself." And he says that for American readers, Baudelaire is "compromised" by having made himself Poe's disciple. His dismissal of Baudelaire is not altogether glib, however. He makes an interesting comparison between the French poet and Hawthorne to the effect that the former "knew

de Goncourt, who shared Baudelaire's aesthetic aims as well as what Auerbach characterizes as his "sensory fascination of the ugly, the repulsive, and the morbid" [87] James wrote in 1877 that his "fault is not that he is serious or historical or scientific or instructive, but that he is intolerably unclean." [88]

Such a remark, in view of James's own proclivity toward if not the "ugly" at least the strange, the extreme, the bizarre, the "perverse" on the one hand, and defeat, loss, destruction, renunciation on the other—qualities that among others have led me to characterize his imagination as "negative"—is remarkable. As is his distaste for that poet of "radical evil," Baudelaire. But what is even more remarkable is the moralistic ambience to the term "unclean"—coming from a man who would himself twenty years later be called "disgusting" for the things he exposed children to in his fiction. An analogous kind of comment on *Madame Bovary*, made in 1874, is equally odd but finally, when we try to characterize James's contradictory affinities in order to place him historically, instructive:

"Madame Bovary," we confess, has always seemed to us a great work, and capable really of being applied to educational purposes. It is an elaborate picture of vice, but it represents it

---

evil not by experience, not as something within himself, but by contemplation and curiosity, as something outside himself," in comparison with Hawthorne, "who felt the thing at its source, deep in the human consciousness." *French Poets and Novelists* (New York, 1904), pp. 60–62.

[87] *Mimesis*, p. 440.

[88] *Literary Reviews and Essays: On American, English, and French Literature*, ed. Albert Mordell (New York, 1957), p. 165.

as so indefeasibly commingled with misery that in a really enlightened system of education it would form exactly the volume to put into the hands of young persons in whom vicious tendencies had been distinctly perceived, and who were wavering as to which way they should let the balance fall.[89]

These remarks, of course, date from a time when James was just beginning his career as a novelist, more than a quarter of a century before his Prince was to murmur, "Everything's terrible, cara—in the heart of man" in the novel where "good" and "evil" become so radically juxtaposed that all distinction between them crumbles, which is to say that as categories they cease to exist. Nevertheless, these early attitudes in their tendentious, almost pompous, and certainly unexamined conventionality betray the side of James that seemed to remain frozen in the official "false consciousness" of Victorian culture.[90] He is of course quite correct in saying (in the Baudelaire piece) that "morality" is hardly something you can put into or take out of fiction as if it were a colored liquid, but later he was to define that term more subtly, in terms of intensity, the evocation of "felt life," and the quality and capacity of the artist's sensibility—*not* in terms of "vice" or the "thousand indecencies and impuri-

[89] *Ibid.* p. 146.

[90] Moreover, they persisted: "Oscar Wilde is here—an unclean beast" (to Godkin, 1882). Leon Edel, *Henry James: The Middle Years, 1882–1895* (New York, 1962), p. 31. Thirteen years later James was somewhat more temperate on Wilde: "He was never in the smallest degree interesting to me—but this hideous human history has made him so—in a manner" (to Edmund Gosse, April 8, 1895). *The Selected Letters of Henry James,* ed. Leon Edel (New York, 1955), p. 147.

ties of life" that make art seem "base and hungry, starving, desperate . . . as one who has wasted her substance in riotous living" if she deals with (or in James's word "overhauls") them! [91] The later definition makes room for a preoccupation with "impurities" and evil, since the standards have shifted from the content of the vision to its sincerity, complexity, and intelligence: "No good novel will ever proceed from a superficial mind; that seems to me an axiom which, for the artist in fiction, will cover all needful moral ground." [92]

James thus embodied some of the ferocious contradictions of his age and undermined others. But though he was our first great experimentalist in the art of fiction, he never reached the point of deliberate innovation and breaking with the past that characterized the early moderns like Proust, Joyce, Woolf, and Faulkner, nor were his formal experimentations accompanied by an explicit metaphysic. Only after the outbreak of World War I, near the end of his life, did he consciously dissociate himself from and impugn the past, giving vent to nihilistic and despairing sentiments about the treachery of history, civilization, and nature. He never seemed to have faced the degree to which he had long since sloughed off some of the more comforting presuppositions of his time and taken up residence in the uncertain and ambiguous universe of the present.

All form implies a metaphysic, whether or not it is conscious or easily discernible. As Robbe-Grillet, Ortega,

[91] *Literary Reviews,* p. 162.

[92] "The Art of Fiction," *The Great Critics: An Anthology of Literary Criticism,* 3d ed. James Harry Smith and Edd Winfield Parks (New York, 1951), p. 669.

and others have pointed out, the typical nineteenth-century novel was predicated upon and projected an image of "a stable, coherent, continuous, unequivocal, entirely decipherable universe"—an image that was revealed by and implicit in such technical aspects of these works as "systematic use of the past tense and the third person, unconditional adoption of chronological development, linear plots, regular trajectory of the passions, impulse of each episode toward a conclusion." [93]

The "order" that was the form of the work was a symbol of the "order" posited of the universe. In the great Victorian novelists, this connection and the world view itself were largely unconscious. In contrast, in the modern novel, what is lacking is not the "anecdote" but "only its character of certainty [and therefore that of the world image implied by it], its tranquility, its innocence." [94] The uncertainty is, moreover, explicit and conscious. Speaking of our "unintelligible and limited universe," Camus writes that "today people despair of true knowledge. . . . This heart within me I can feel, and I judge that it exists. This world I can touch, and I likewise judge that it exists. There ends all my knowledge, and the rest is construction." [95]

The form of works like *Nausea* and *The Stranger* stands in deliberate ironic juxtaposition to the formless, irrational, unintelligible, contingent reality that these novels posit. It is this ironical structuring of events that Robbe-Grillet misses when he charges both Sartre and Camus with a "fatal [and to him heretical] complicity" [96]

---

[93] *For a New Novel*, p. 32.   [94] *Ibid.*, p. 33.
[95] *The Myth of Sisyphus, The Modern Tradition*, p. 826.
[96] *For a New Novel*, p. 62.

with the universe. Just as nausea was, so absurdity is "really a form of tragic humanism. It is not an observation of the separation between man and things. . . . The world [in *The Stranger*] is accused of complicity in a murder." [97]

This is simply wrong. The conjunction of the man overly sensitive to the sun, with a gun in his hand, in oppressively hot surroundings, and a waiting victim, is accidental. These figures in conjunction create a design, but it is one without meaning; it has or consists merely of formal properties, and that is all.

What the design does (and this is reinforced by the book's elaborate and rather tediously obvious metaphorical structure superimposed upon the chronological one— the pattern formed by the images of light, heat, and glare, increasing in intensity, climaxed at the murder scene) is to create the *appearance* of complicity where there in fact is none, the illusion that the murder was brought about by the heartless or diabolic intent of some intelligent force in the universe. The illusion, moreover, is intensified by the way in which not only nature but all events—Meursault's chance encounters, the witnesses and their interpretations of the meaning of his gestures, timing—*seem* to conspire to condemn him. But clearly implicit in the idea of the "absurd" is the human need to ascribe purposeful design (even if it is malicious) to the accidental. "This world," Camus writes, "in itself is not reasonable, that is all that can be said. But what is absurd is the confrontation of this irrational and the wild longing for clarity whose call echoes in the human heart." [98]

[97] *Ibid.*, p. 64.
[98] *The Myth of Sisyphus, The Modern Tradition*, p. 827.

The design (the pattern of intensifying light and heat) woven by Meursault's susceptibilities out of random occurrences is as objectively meaningless—that is to say false, fictional—as that of the witnesses (who ascribe various "meanings" to certain of his appearances, words, responses). The hero and his antagonists are all poets, creating the illusion of meaning, in this case of a demonic nature, where there is none. As in *The Sacred Fount* all that is required is some kind of closed system that seems to explain the facts (one such system Meursault divines when he realizes he is to be executed "because he didn't weep at his mother's funeral").

The emotional effect of the work is in part due to the ironic contrast between the logic (which suggests a meaning, a "point," an explanation) of these designs and their fictionality. In plays of Genet's like *The Balcony, The Blacks,* or *The Screens* this process is carried a step further by deliberate assaults on the audience's suspension of disbelief. These are made possible by a variety of techniques such as the juxtaposition of real and painted objects for props (the function of the former being "to establish a contrast between [their] own reality and the objects that are drawn" [99]); the successive postulation and abolition (within the confines of the play) of a distinction between a series of "real" worlds and make-believe ones the characters choose to construct; explicit suggestion that the fakery of the stage is superseded only by that of life, and so on. These techniques are aimed not only at first invoking then breaking down the ordinary distinction between illusion and reality, but also at

[99] *The Screens*, trans. Bernard Frechtman (New York, 1962), p. 10.

making that breakdown conscious *and* in concretizing or, as Ortega would say, "worldifying" it. We are forced to experience the contradiction between expectations traditionally appropriate to the fictional on the one hand and the real on the other, and this clash is the point: there is a joke somewhere. Art is mocking both itself and life, and in particular its own capacity to suggest order and significance through illusion, and is insisting that we recognize —though that does not mean we have to cease to admire it—as mere illusion.

Though James shares with moderns like Genet and Camus the assumption that art is structured in a way that life is not, he does not, as they do, deliberately undercut its order and coherency or play it off against the disorder and absurdity of life. He recognizes the *arbitrariness* of form—that "geometry of his own" which the artist constructs—but the recognition only occasionally (as in *The Sacred Fount*) entails self-mockery, and certainly entails neither anxiety nor anguish. On the contrary, he accepts the discrepancy between art and life as a matter of course and, at the same time, with all seriousness and dedication in his role as "the Master."

He is a great ironist, but his irony by and large does not spring from or concern itself with a consciousness of his own aesthetic assumptions, processes, or artifacts. And though his books in some respects betray a much more radical ontological stance than he seemed conscious of or ever directly expressed until his heartbreak and disillusion upon the outbreak of World War I,[100] in other respects

[100] From a letter to Rhoda Broughton, August 10, 1914: "Black and hideous to me is the tragedy that gathers, and I'm sick beyond cure to have lived on to see it. You and I, the ornaments of our

they remain rooted in the past. The universe postulated by his fiction, for example, is not only an ordered one—this he shares with the Victorian novelists—but, like Hardy's, it is almost "overdetermined." In James's world, the contingent becomes the necessary; his designs are as wrought and as taut as those in *The Stranger,* but we are meant in his case to believe in the design, not perceive it as a kind of ghastly illusion that toys with our sense of coherence.

There is, nevertheless, behind the richness of texture, the sensuous particularity, the superb and often satirical discriminations of national styles and manners so characteristic of his work, plenty of the ghastly lurking in James's lustrous visions. For—unlike in the Victorian novel, with its ultimately serene triumph of the "good"— the order that is seen to operate is a negative, a diabolic one, a geometry of destruction, an order, as he wrote in

---

generation, should have been spared this wreck of our belief that through the long years we had seen civilization grow and the worst become impossible. . . . It seems to me to *undo* everything, everything that was ours, in the most horrible retroactive way . . . and the huge shining indifference of Nature strikes a chill to the heart and makes me wonder of what abysmal mystery, or villainy indeed, such a cruel smile is the expression."

To William Roughhead, September 30, 1914: " . . . so utterly broken off and disconnected, and all in a night, has become every blest old fact of the happy world made for our stricken sight, as we turn it back, by the simple . . . circumstance of its not having been a perpetual black nightmare. However, *my* dark dream has lights, lurid, but extremely vivid; I never *wanted* to live on to see the collapse of so many fond faiths, which makes all the past, with this hideous card all the while up its sleeve, seem now a long treachery, an unthinkable humbug." *The Selected Letters of Henry James,* ed. Leon Edel (New York, 1955), pp. 218–219, 220.

the Preface to *The Wings of the Dove,* of "Fates, powers conspiring to a sinister end and, with their command of means, finally achieving it." [101]

In this respect, the "consolations" of form become a moot point, and belong to the order of comfort Meursault invokes in his cell when he cries out in rage to the priest that it is "better to burn than to disappear." If any order—even an order of pain—is better than none or the mocking semblance of one, then James's vision is more "positive" than some of our contemporaries whose mockery he helped prepare for by his "play" with form, his delight in the perverse, and his demonic capacity to render reality from varied, contrasting, conflicting, perspectives.

[101] *The Art of the Novel,* p. 290.

CHAPTER II

The Wings of the Dove

THE CENTRAL situations in most of James's novels are very similar: conflict is brought about by two characteristics shared by protagonists and antagonists alike—a greediness or hunger to have everything that life might offer, coupled with an unwillingness to accept or possibly even to acknowledge limitations to the realization of their desires. And yet there always are limitations: the execution *is* confined, and in the Jamesian fictional world with more formal rigor even than in life itself. In this world, experience is limited by being polarized, most often into the extremes represented by the European and American ways of life. And this European-American antithesis is as much a symbolic construct of impossibilities as it is of possibilities. If the face of the American coin is innocence and energy, fortune and freedom, "old heads and . . . young morals," as Chad Newman reflects, its back is unworldliness and washtubs, a general bewilderment at the arithmetic of art, culture, and taste. Similarly, if to be a European is to be, in contrast to this, "a master of all the distinctively social virtues and a votary of all the agreeable sensations," it is to be at the same time corrupt, to be a possessor of "morals the most grizzled and wrinkled." [1]

In the early novels (*Roderick Hudson, The American, The Europeans*) someone always tries—and always fails—to annex the virtues of both civilizations without paying the price of the vices of each; in other words, to remake the conditions of his world.[2] Such an effort, attended by such a failure, is also the paradigm of the dramatic situation in the late novels. In these, however, the antitheses are more complex, the "goods" and "bads" more manifold. But the same hunger and yearning for the best of all possible worlds continue to provide the motivating principle for the interaction of the characters. In *The Wings of the Dove,* for example, both Merton and Kate defy the logical and moral restrictions that seem to be inherent in their situation. Merton will have Kate and his honor too; Kate will have Merton and a fortune too. Yet in each case circumstances decree that the choice of one of these precludes the other. The plot issues from the characters' defiance of this dictate, from their yearning and greed for both alternatives, which set into

[1] Henry James, *The American,* New York ed., Vol. II (New York, 1907), p. 134.

[2] See Chapter I for a more detailed discussion of this matter with respect to *The Europeans.*

motion the deepest concerns of the novel: pursuit and possession, perjury and blame, the ultimate despising of what one has sought because of what one has done to oneself in seeking it.

In the broadest sense the novel is an anatomy of guilt; of the causes, then the consequences, of deliberate, conscious violation of another human being's existence for the sake of personal gain. Each half of the book deals in a general way with one of these two aspects of the subject, so that the major structural break that takes place at the end of Book V corresponds with the shift in thematic focus from the genesis of guilt to its consequences.

James's own image for the novel's subject is a medal hanging free so that "its obverse and its reverse, its face and its back, would beautifully become optional for the spectator." The medal's face is the "stricken state" of Milly Theale, its back "the state of others as affected by her"[3] and, one might add, as affected by themselves in relation to her. As the events of the novel play themselves out, the word "stricken" takes on new meaning, referring finally not so much to the peril to her health as to the blow given to her will to live in spite of it when she discovers the real connection between Kate and Merton. Similarly, the way in which others are "affected by" Milly means one thing at the outset of the story, quite another as she begins in fact to be deceived. In the beginning Kate and Merton are affected by the possibility of using her, in the end by the actuality of having done so and the nightmarish difference that this makes. The emotional complex is shifting and varied, moving for them from

[3] Henry James, *The Art of the Novel: Critical Prefaces*, ed. R. P. Blackmur (New York, 1962), p. 294.

greed to remorse, from activity to paralysis and, for Milly, from ignorance to knowledge—which in this context is to say from hope to agony.

The real subject of the book in other words is a dynamic one. It is neither the deceived nor the deceiver who is studied but rather the changing relationship between the two and the phenomenon itself of manipulation; of the circumstances that give rise to it and of the effects it has upon both victim and victimizer. This is what James means, I think, when he speaks, in reference to his narrative method, of scarcely remembering "a case . . . in which the curiosity of 'beginning far back,' as far back as possible, and even of going, to the same tune, far 'behind,' that is behind the face of the subject, was to assert itself with less scruple." [4] So he writes that "though my regenerate young New Yorker, and what might depend on her, should form my centre, my circumference was every whit as treatable. . . . One began, in the event, with the outer ring, approaching the centre thus by narrowing circumvallations." [5]

His "outer ring" then is the state of the other characters as affected by Milly and by what she represents at the outset of the novel. It is what he begins with, even though Book I ostensibly deals just with Kate and her family. From the ground laid in that book Milly is only, in James's words, "superficially" absent. Kate is shown under the pressure of various circumstances creating for her a series of dilemmas, all of which, however different in certain respects, have one thing in common: they would not exist if Kate had a fortune like Milly's. These circumstances weave into a web of considerable precision, and if the

[4] *Ibid.*, p. 295.   [5] *Ibid.*, p. 294.

moth is superficially absent, the spider is waiting; one might say that a general invitation has been issued. Something of the sense of this is what James means when he speaks of having intended Milly's predicament to be created "promptly" and built up "solidly, so that it should have for us as much as possible its ominous air of awaiting her." [6]

The predicament is certainly solid. There is an inexorable and formal irony in the very confluence of events operating on and within Kate that is reminiscent in its way of Hardy. By various vague and nameless deeds Kate's father has brought the family, which includes the four small children of her widowed sister, into dishonor and financial collapse. Her wealthy aunt is willing to rescue Kate on the explicit condition that she renounce all contact with her father and on the unspoken condition that she marry a man of the aunt's choice. Kate herself is beautiful, proud, poor but covetous of wealth, and in love with a penniless man not of her aunt's choice. She is also painfully conscious of the responsibilities and obligations, the silken cords of familial relations, and "the part, not always either uplifting or sweetening, that the bond of blood might play in one's life." [7] She is not free from this bond—as Milly so pre-eminently is—either in fact or, more important, in feeling. "That's all my virtue" she murmurs to Densher, "—a narrow little family feeling. I've a small stupid piety—I don't know what to call it" (XIX, 71). Finally, she occupies a unique position within the family complex: with her youth, her pride, her

---

[6] *Ibid.*

[7] Henry James, *The Wings of the Dove*, New York ed. (New York, 1909), XIX, 32. Subsequent citations are to this edition.

presence, and the magnetism that makes her appear "more 'dressed,' often, with fewer accessories, than other women, or less dressed, should occasion require, with more" (XIX, 5), she is the one piece of solid collateral the disgraced and distressed family possesses, the one tangible asset whose worth to them is the price it will bring at barter. And she knows it. Lionel Croy has few pleasures. Like Gilbert Osmond in *The Portrait of a Lady*, he is concerned with appearances and wears the mask of propriety but feels almost nothing. Yet he does take pleasure, she realizes, in the fact "that she was handsome, that she was in her way a tangible value" (XIX, 9). And later she repeats to Densher, "My position's a value, a great value, for them both. . . . It's *the* value—the only one they have. . . . It makes me ask myself if I've any right to personal happiness, any right to anything but to be as rich and overflowing, as smart and shining, as I can be made" (XIX, 71).

So the theme of manipulation, of tampering, of regarding a fellow human being not as a person but as an object for use is present from the beginning of the novel, more horrifying perhaps because of its context within the family setting, where the distortion and reversal of roles are so severe, the primary responsibility of who nurtures whom so askew, that the situation takes on almost cannibalistic overtones: a family party feeding off the younger daughter.

The purpose of these opening chapters according to James was to "account" for Kate: "The image of her so compromised and compromising father was all effectively to have pervaded her life, was in a certain particular way to have tampered with her spring; by which I mean that the shame and the irritation and the depression, the general poisonous influence of him, were to have been *shown*." "They weren't shown," James feels; instead the author's "poor word of honour has *had* to pass muster for the show." [8] And it is true that Lionel Croy's compromising influence does not really seem to have very much to do with Kate's deepest possibilities and energies. But it does not matter; it is not a serious flaw. When we first view Kate gazing into the mirror, the impact of her beauty, vitality, and power speaks for itself. She does not need "accounting for." Her personality with both its resources and its susceptibilities, its passion and its narcissism, is one of the givens of the novel, the concern of which as a study of human guilt is phenomenological rather than psychological. To the extent that the novel is concerned with causes, it is as they exist in the combination of character and circumstance, not as they relate to the origins of character itself. And though James is one of the great scholars of human motives, his interest is in their processes: in the effects, the implications, the reverberations of self-interest and not in its psycho-dynamics.

Some guilt by association does touch Kate: her sister is abject, her father is full of "folly and cruelty and wickedness" (XIX, 64), her aunt is "unscrupulous and immoral" (XIX, 31). It is sufficient for the evil of the day that Kate exists in contiguity with them, that she is the prime object of their various desires, and that she recognizes this and even partially acknowledges its justice. By so doing of course she accepts not only their right to use her but also, by extension, anyone's right

[8] *The Art of the Novel,* pp. 297, 298.

to use anyone who might be in a position to be useful. The acceptance of this principle is the primary distortion of human values in the novel, and it operates on a number of levels,[9] reversing the meaning even of ordinary terms of moral discourse. Thus Kate is under pressure from all the members of her family not to be "selfish," that is not to marry a penniless man or, to put it another way, not to marry the man she loves since he not only is penniless but also feels that the "innermost fact . . . of his own consciousness" is his "private inability to believe he should ever be rich" (XIX, 62).

It is not merely through the eyes of her family, however, that Kate regards herself as an object to be put to use, but through her own eyes as well. Looking at herself in the mirror, she meditates upon the possibility of at least a partial escape from ruin—escape implicit in the fact that she is "agreeable to see." And she is aware of her power: "If she saw more things than her fine face in the dull glass of her father's lodgings she might have seen that after all she was not herself a fact in the collapse. She did n't hold herself cheap, she did n't make for misery" (XIX, 5–6). To an extent her vision of herself is one with that of her family: they don't judge her cheap either. The difference is in her intense personal pride, which is

[9] Most of the relationships in the book can be looked at from the point of view of who is using whom: Kate's father, sister, and sisters-in-law try to recover their ruined fortune by pressuring her to accept Aunt Maud's offer to "do for" her; Aunt Maud in turn has had Kate "marked from far back" as the means by which she can realize her own social ambitions if Kate under her tutelage marries properly; through Kate's countermanipulations and Densher's passive assistance, Aunt Maud herself becomes the one who is used; and everyone—including Lord Mark, the subtle parasite Eugenio, and even, it could be argued, Susie—uses Milly.

reflected in an extension of her self-identification to the "precious" family name, the debasing of which causes her shame and a quality of remorse they themselves do not share. With a certain horror, Kate sees her sister's abjectness, watches her "instinctively neglect nothing that would make for her submission to their aunt" (XIX, 34), realizes that Marion's lust for profit is "quite oblivious" of dignity, honor, and pride.

One of the most characteristic traits of James's imagination is to see life in terms of mutually exclusive possibilities and negative alternatives. The typical problem faced by his characters is not so much a choice as a dilemma, in which any decision means some major sacrifice, capitulation, or surrender. And for Kate the dilemma rapidly becomes acute; she has accepted her position, even to the extent of questioning her own right to personal happiness, as the family pawn. At the same time it is only she who can or cares to preserve their collective dignity. To preserve it means not to be abject, but not to be abject means in turn "to prefer an ideal of behaviour—than which nothing ever was more selfish—to the possibility of stray crumbs for the four small creatures" (XIX, 34). So that any way she turns, something, and something important, stands to be lost.

Her one attempt to maintain her spiritual freedom, her integrity, literally her wholeness, of self is her initial offer to her father to stick by him, with or without Densher, and renounce Aunt Maud. This is the first and last unequivocally moral gesture Kate makes in the course of the novel, and part of the inexorability of the patterning of circumstances spoken of earlier lies in its never being allowed to become a genuine option for her. The irony is intensified by the fact that of all the various pressures operating upon and within her, not the least is that of her own "dire accessibility to pleasure" from material things, from "trimmings and lace . . . ribbons and silk and velvet . . . charming quarters" (XIX, 28).[10] It is an accessibility that makes her feel in danger; in the face of the temptation offered by Aunt Maud, Kate likens herself to "a trembling kid . . . sure sooner or later to be introduced into the cage of the lioness" (XIX, 30). Yet the source of the danger is internal not external, and Aunt Maud's imagined ferocity is an image for Kate of some possibility within herself that she dreads and that Milly too is soon to dread, recognizing after an interview with Kate that "she had felt herself alone with a creature who paced like a panther" (XIX, 282).

The intensity of the temptation Kate feels is a measure of the meaning of her gesture to her father. It is no empty offer, but an effort to redeem herself in advance from herself, from what she so clearly senses she might do, and by doing, become. "I did it," she cries to Densher, "to save myself—to escape" (XIX, 69). To save herself and "the precious name" she is willing at this juncture to give up both love and a possible fortune—a willingness, perhaps understandably, she never demonstrates again.

Given, then, the nature of her own character in the context of circumstances that surround it, there is no set of alternative actions that does not represent a dilemma for Kate. She does not want to give up Densher, yet she

[10] In respect to material things of course, her susceptibility is one with her family's; it is only their abjectness in the face of it that she loathes. There is a sense in which their whole relationship with her parodies the forces that in a subtler way most motivate Kate.

does not want to be poor, and she would be poor if she married him. She especially does not want, after the example of the Misses Condrips' who spend their days sniffing out dregs of gossip that might somehow be turned to their financial advantage, to be both poor and unmarried. She does not want to be dishonorable. She does not want to see her family's fortune and honor remain in the mud. She does not want to sacrifice her personal—and familial—dignity to regain that fortune, yet she does not want to have to maintain that dignity at the cost of taking crumbs away from babes. If she maintains her integrity she sacrifices her family to poverty and, equally to the point, herself as well. So that the choice of any one alternative means the surrender of the other possibilities. And that in turn means the renunciation of her ideal self-image, because that image is precisely a composite of all the possibilities: it is Kate wealthy, dignified, of proud name, charitable in her munificence, and married to Merton Densher.

The one sacrifice on the altar of this vision is her morality. Not the appearance of it, since to seem untouchable and beyond scandal, to have the aura of propriety, is an intrinsic part of her ideal portrait of herself. But certainly the fact of it. So she tells Densher she sees as her one danger the possibility "of doing something base" (XIX, 72). It is not the danger of "chucking him," as he suggests: "I *shan't* sacrifice you. Don't cry out till you're hurt. I shall sacrifice nobody and nothing, and that's just my situation, that I want and that I shall try for everything" (XIX, 73).

Kate's cry of yearning is to be echoed in one form or another by all of the characters, "good" and "bad" alike, in the late novels. Her situation, that of a person whose longings will recognize no limits and yet who is caught up in circumstances that are unusually limiting, is a microcosm of the fundamental situation James deals with again and again. His imagination so orders reality that the possibilities for happiness that face each character inevitably have an either-or quality about them, and yet the characters are all the kind of people for whom the alternative to the fulfillment of their desires is an empty, pointless existence. And it is in terms of these two extremes that James persistently examines the meaning and significance of "morality." For Kate, the pendulum has swung full swing: if initially she was willing to renounce everything to preserve her spiritual safety, she is now willing to surrender that safety to preserve everything else. In a sense what she does is simply to reject the logical premise of her situation—the premise that she is in a dilemma, that she must choose between one thing and another. But her one peril, that of doing something base, is by definition also a peril to someone else. The shifts in her feeling and attitudes toward herself can be reduced to a series of propositions about the nature of the relationship between self-gratification and morality, and the limits on each imposed by the other. Kate's situation, as she sees it, is such that the price of absolute morality is absolute self-renunciation; the price of partial morality is partial self-renunciation; and finally, the reward of immorality is total self-gratification. It is the novel's concern to disprove this last proposition, but the rigor of her "logic" is nonetheless one of the forces motivating the subsequent events.

This fact, together with the fact that the possession of a

fortune is the *sine qua non* of her vision, constitutes the basis of Milly's predicament, and is why it has indeed "its ominous air of awaiting her." Milly has a fortune, Kate needs one; Milly is passive and gentle—a dove; Kate is restless and ruthless—a panther. In addition not only is Milly mortally ill while Kate is vibrantly alive, but also Milly's one English acquaintance happens to be Merton Densher, and she happens to be susceptible to his attractions. Thus every element in Milly's situation has its opposite correspondence in Kate's, and the predicament of the former is a function or extension of the predicament of the latter; it is its logical outgrowth.

One could indeed say that much of the energy of the novel is logistical, rhetorical, dialectical. And clearly both the strengths and the weaknesses of the book are in some important way tied up with this fact. The structuring of the plot, for example, the way the initial dramatic situation is conceived and set up, is characterized by a high degree of formal balance and antithesis, correspondences and oppositions. The way in which what Milly needs and what Milly has to offer so neatly dovetail with what Kate needs, and also has to offer, is almost too good to be true. Or too painful to be bearable, which is the effect James intended. The "soul of drama," he writes, ". . . is the portrayal, as we know, of a catastrophe determined in spite of oppositions. My young woman would *herself* be the opposition—to the catastrophe announced by the associated Fates." [11]

That is, the effect of the remorseless logic of the combined circumstances of the two girls is precisely the feeling of impending catastrophe—and catastrophe that is

[11] *The Art of the Novel*, p. 290.

inevitable, unavoidable, inexorable. Whatever one might argue about the apparent improbabilities, coincidences, even patnesses of the initial situation in the novel, the result is one of ironic contrast, of heightened tension and expectation. There is something ruthless in the manipulation of the events, to be sure, but that very fact contributes to the intensity of the emotional effect, the sense of dread and pity, the feeling of the inevitable mockery and destruction of the deep yearning for life that is so profound a part of Milly's makeup.

The effect is not merely dramatic; it is almost diabolic. There is something reminiscent of a hellish chess game in the book's presentation of the mathematics of narrowing alternatives, in which the loser of the game not only does not know she is losing, she does not even know she is playing. James has an almost Satanic instinct for situation; indeed much of his power as a novelist lies in his remorselessness in this respect.

Remorseless in his delineation of character too, he is one of the great pathologists of human nature we have in modern fiction. His ability to cast a cold eye on a whole spectrum of moral sickness and to present it without flinching is one of the paradoxes of a sensibility that in many respects evaded the direct confrontation of powerful emotion. In the midst of the yearning and separation that are characteristic motifs of his imagination is this preoccupation with the darker aspects of the human psyche, a preoccupation characterized by the degree to which the author seems close to and unfearful of its concerns rather than detached or distant from them. "What bothers Gide most in James' characters," writes Matthiessen, "is the excessive functioning of their analytical powers, whereas . . . 'all the shaggy, tangled undergrowth, all the wild darkness [is absent.] . . .' But in works as different as *The Turn of the Screw* and *The Wings of the Dove,* James showed an extraordinary command of his own kind of darkness, not the darkness of passion, but the darkness of moral evil." [12]

The characters in *The Wings of the Dove* form a spectrum ranging from evil to moral mediocrity: Lionel Croy, who had "no truth in him. . . . He dealt out lies as he might the cards from the greasy old pack for the game of diplomacy to which you were to sit down with him" (XIX, 7); Aunt Maud, "Britannia of the Market Place," who, in addition to her "florid philistinism . . . fantastic furniture and heaving bosom, the false gods of her taste and false notes of her talk," was "unscrupulous and immoral" (XIX, 30–31); Marion, "grown red and almost fat" (XIX, 37), and whose abjectness and desire to profit are oblivious of any dignity; the Misses Condrips, who "lived in a deeper hole than Marion, but . . . kept their ear to the ground . . . spent their days in prowling" (XIX, 43); Susan Shepherd, who "had now no life to lead; and she honestly believed that she was thus supremely equipped for leading Milly's own" (XIX, 113), and in whose view "it was life enough simply to feel her companion's feelings" (XIX, 115); Lord Mark, "bald . . . and slightly stale" (XIX, 151), to whom Milly remarks, "You're *blasé,* but you're not enlightened. You're familiar with everything, but conscious really of nothing. What I mean is that you've no imagination" (XIX, 162), and who "pointed to nothing; which was very possibly just a sign of his real cleverness, one of those that the really clever

[12] *Henry James: The Major Phase* (New York, 1944), pp. 93–94.

had in common with the really void" (XIX, 178); the "great" Eugenio, "recommended by grand-dukes and Americans," who was "a swindler finished to the finger-tips . . . for ever carrying one well-kept Italian hand to his heart and plunging the other straight into her pocket, which, as she had instantly observed him to recognise, fitted it like a glove" (XX, 132–33); Sir Luke Strett of the "thousand knives": "What *was* he in fact but patient, what was she [Milly] but physician, from the moment she embraced once for all the necessity, adopted once for all the policy, of saving him alarms about her subtlety?" (XX, 125).

This, aside from the protagonists, constitutes the cast of *The Wings of the Dove:* the vulgar and the vicarious, the abject and the empty, the snoopers and swindlers, the relentless and the helpless. It is on the whole a considerably tamer list of characters than is to be found in that problematic group of novels that immediately precede the major works: *What Maisie Knew, The Awkward Age,* and *The Sacred Fount,* and furthermore the comic and satiric note[13] in the mode of their presentation is obvious. Still, it is a society less of fools than of knaves, most of whom, to the degree of their talents, have in common the fine art of calculated self-gain.

It is the society in which the gentle dove, the princess, the heiress of all the ages finds herself, small wonder, a

[13] Kate, in near despair over her father's rejection of her offer to forsake all others and go with him, exclaims: "I wish there were some one here who might serve—for any contingency—as a witness that I *have* put it to you that I'm ready to come."

"Would you like me [her father asked] to call the landlady?" (XIX, 20–21).

"success." Its keynote, a somewhat ravenous mutual parasitism (not symbiosis), is sounded almost from the beginning, when Lord Mark, at Milly's first London dinner party, after pronouncing her a success, "pleasantly" remarks that Mrs. Lowder will, however, get back her money: "He could say it too—which was singular—without affecting her either as vulgar or as 'nasty'; and he had soon explained himself by adding: 'Nobody here, you know, does anything for nothing.'" (XIX, 160). This explicit note of warning to Milly is sounded twice again, by Kate herself. The first instance is soon after the dinner, when Kate explains that Lord Mark himself is no more indifferent to himself than Aunt Maud is to herself," for he was working Lancaster Gate for all it was worth: just as it was, no doubt, working *him*, and just as the working and the worked were in London, as one might explain, the parties to every relation" (XIX, 178). And strangest of all, Kate adds, is the "happy understanding" that "the worker in one connexion was the worked in another" (XIX, 179). But on the subject of Milly's own paying role, Kate declines discussion: it is to be taken for granted that "Milly would pay a hundred per cent—and even to the end, doubtless, through the nose" (XIX, 180).

The *tone* of the remarks—which might mislead, even amuse, someone of much greater sophistication than Milly [14]—is of course calculated for amusement; first of all for the narcissistic amusement of the inner circle in which the question of anyone's being misled by it simply does

[14] The tone is summarized by Milly: "These were the fine facilities, pleasantries, ironies, all these luxuries of gossip and philosophies of London and of life, and they became quickly, between the pair, the common form of talk" (XIX, 180).

not exist. The game of treating Milly as if she were a fully initiated member of the circle is an added refinement, the ironical contrast between their words and her response (or their awareness and her innocence) providing a source of mild sadistic pleasure. In itself this is not entirely heinous: there can be something extraordinarily irritating about total gullibility—especially in the possessor of an immense fortune, dazzled by her social "success" but unaware that it is a function of the fortune, and unaware too that in proper perspective it is she and not they who should be dispensing the favor of "acceptance." Her obvious and abysmal ignorance of the *kind* of society into which she has made her triumphant debut is a further irritant: Lord Mark is a penniless *inutile* aristocrat, Mrs. Lowder is a moderately well heeled, status-seeking Philistine. These two revolve in each other's orbits because of the obvious possibility of bartering goods to their mutual benefit. Yet of all this, Milly, with both status and millions (she is "the girl with the background, the girl with the crown of old gold" [XIX, 109]), is oblivious.

It is only in conjunction with the other complex functions it serves that the tone of the social intercourse of this group becomes sinister. It is geared toward the flattery, seduction, and deception of Milly. And the mask of frankness is a means to all these ends: it is flattering to be told what is "really" going on behind the glittering social façade; seduction is a process accomplished by effecting the substitution of one set of values for another, less rigorous and more "honest" to the infinitely varied nature of man; deception occurs when appearances are made misleading. In this case the logic roughly is that no one really so out for himself as Kate and Lord Mark describe would admit it, hence the admission is a kind of sophisticated joke, a "pleasantry."

And it is perfectly true that in a society which condemned stepping on others to advance oneself, no one would admit to it. But it is not that kind of society. It does not value honor and honesty and selflessness, but only their appearance. It does value material wealth and social status, and gives both tacit and open approval to any means utilized to obtain them.

Milly's fundamental error of judgment with respect to her English acquaintances is her failure to recognize this inversion of values, her assumption that she and they speak a common moral language. In fact nothing could be further from the truth: there are two separate grammars here and, as in any two widely different languages, different assumptions about the nature and significance of reality.

Up to a point, as we have seen, her error is the result of the deliberate deception practiced upon her, and she is therefore blameless. But with Kate's second warning to Milly, the complexion of events alters significantly: the panther reveals itself for a moment. To Milly's comment on the remarkable kindness of Aunt Maud, Kate exclaims: "Oh but she has . . . plenty of use for you! You put her in, my dear, more than you put her out. You don't half see it, but she has clutched your petticoat. You can do anything—you can do, I mean, lots that *we* can't. You're an outsider, independent and standing by yourself; you're not hideously relative to tiers and tiers of others. . . . We're of no use to you—it's decent to tell you. You'd be of use to us, but that's a different matter. My honest advice to you would be . . . to drop us while you can." She continues with a denunciation of Susan Stringham for having let Milly in to the mess, and when Milly protests, "And yet without Susie I should n't have had *you*," Kate flashes back, "Oh, you may very well loathe me yet!" (XIX, 281–282).

Milly's story is one of resisting until too late, and in spite of reiterated warnings, knowledge that she should have accepted; a story of not seeing. She is practiced upon by others "for interests and advantages, from motives and points of view, of their own," and these "promptings" from others, James writes, constitute "contributively, her sum of experience, represent to her somehow, in good faith or in bad, what she should have *known*." [15]

Of course, Milly's stake in not knowing is very great indeed. Part of James's dramatic genius consists of his diabolic sense for situations in which the negative significance of alternative choices for the characters is stronger than the positive. Either way for Milly now is a matter of life or death, or rather, death is the probability, life only a possibility. One of the most powerful things in the novel is the portrayal of her resistance to the insights that in fact she has again and again; long before Kate's outburst of frankness, Milly has sensed dangers, "sinister motives," "brutality," "the not wholly calculable" as well as the potent and magnetic beauty of her friend, the fact that she was "made for great social uses." But even worse, Milly has felt "the hint of pity," first from Kate, then from Sir Luke, then from Aunt Maud, as she is later to feel

[15] *The Art of the Novel,* p. 291.

from Densher, Eugenio, Susie, Lord Mark—from everyone in fact with whom she comes into contact. When
Aunt Maud displays it, independently, Milly takes it as
"the charge of weakness. It was what every one, if she
did n't look out, would soon be saying—'There's something the matter with you!' " (XIX, 270).

The "matter" with her is a complex thing from the point
of view of her London milieu. Kate perceives her stoicism,
her struggle, her fierce pride, but the intense spiritual
beauty, generosity, and hunger of the dying girl fully
become clear only after her death. It is *after* her death
that Merton falls in love with her. Her virtues are not of a
sort to be recognized as such by her English friends; her
innocence, as we have seen, is sport for them; what
deeply interests them about her, what they "revere," is her
fortune, not her inner being. The latter they cannot see
clearly any more than she can see theirs; a blindness is at
work here, to the ultimate woe of all the main actors. But
before Merton, and Kate, are unblinded, Milly is (among
other things) pitied by them; not merely for her illness
but also for her lack of female, animal magnetism, really
of sexuality. Kate, for example, has

a feeling not analysed but divided, a latent impression that
Mildred Theale was not, after all, a person to change places, to
change even chances with. Kate, verily, would perhaps not
quite have known what she meant by this discrimination and
she came near naming it only when she said to herself that,
rich as Milly was, one probably would n't—which was
singular—ever hate her for it. . . . It was n't obscure to her
[Kate] that, without some very particular reason to help, it
might have proved a test of one's philosophy not to be irritated

by a mistress of millions . . . who, as a girl, so easily might have been, like herself, only vague and cruelly female. (XIX, 176)

So that part of what Milly is fighting is the knowledge of the way she is seen by the people closest to her. The reason she resists this, and resists correctly reading their motives, is that to do so would be to learn not so much that they do want her fortune as that they don't want her. Sir Luke has put the responsibility for her life in her own hands; she "could" live if she "would." His prescription against death is to live; he makes it sound simple. To "live" in turn means to fall in love and be loved. She already is in love of course, with the young man the many-splendored Kate keeps failing to mention. At this point, Milly is in possession of all the relevant facts: that Kate and Densher know each other; that Kate envies Milly's money and the freedom it brings; that Densher is poor; that he loves Kate; that Aunt Maud is concerned about their attachment. The one fact anyone actively bothers to deceive her about is the degree of Kate's interest in Merton, but then Milly has the option of drawing her own conclusions about that, except that if she acknowledges the obvious she passes sentence of death upon herself. In short, she can neither afford to see nor afford not to see what the situation really is.

This is an example of James's uncanny instinct for narrowing and negative alternatives, in which any move spells disaster. It is part of what makes him powerful as a dramatist; it is also what can make him nearly unbearable. In the very nature of the situations he constructs, the whole conception of human freedom of action, choice, and hence responsibility, amounts to a bitter farce; it is practically nonexistent. It may be that one reason critics have accused him of "moral unsatisfactoriness" [16] is his almost violent rejection of the notion of free will. Recall his definition of drama as "catastrophe determined in spite of oppositions"—the word "determined" should not pass unnoticed. And what, for example, actually are the alternative courses of action open to the three protagonists? If Kate did not play her game the way she played it, her choices would be either to marry Densher and remain penniless or to marry Lord Mark and remain loveless; equal impossibilities, given her character. Merton has the option of refusing to play Kate's game. If he did, he would preserve his integrity but lose Kate. And the terror that speaks loudest to him is that possibility: "What if I should begin to bore this splendid creature?" Finally Milly, as we have seen, has the option of consciously admitting the implications of what she has observed, sensed, and intuited all along. If she did, she would have spared herself the final humiliation, but she would have died sooner. Kate puts this succinctly to Merton at the end, " 'She never wanted the truth—' —Kate had a high headshake. 'She wanted *you*' " (XX, 326–327).

This is not to suggest that James is unconcerned with these very issues of freedom, will, and responsibility. On the contrary, he is obsessed with them. The concept of "freedom" is the pivotal point of Isabel Archer's character, for example, but the book is about how, thinking she is freely making the choice that will bring her the most freedom, she has in fact been beguiled into making the one that will bring her the least. Milly, too, is profoundly

[16] F. R. Leavis, *The Great Tradition* (Garden City, New York, 1954), p. 205.

concerned with the question of responsibility, but she has a wider, more ironic vision of the various ways of viewing this issue than does Isabel. In a passage of great power, James describes her inward upheaval after she has been told by Sir Luke that whether she lives or dies is up to her: "Grey immensity had somehow of a sudden become her element; grey immensity was what her distinguished friend had, for the moment, furnished her world with and what the question of 'living,' as he put it to her, living by option, by volition, inevitably took on for its immediate face" (XIX, 247). She drives through Regent's Park, and suddenly in her vision identifies her plight with the human plight in general:

Here were benches and smutty sheep; here were idle lads at games of ball, with their cries mild in the thick air; here were wanderers anxious and tired like herself; here doubtless were hundreds of others just in the same box. Their box, their great common anxiety, what was it, in this grim breathing-space, but the practical question of life? They could live if they would; that is, like herself, they had been told so: she saw them all about her, on seats, digesting the information, recognising it again as something in a slightly different shape familiar enough, the blessed old truth that they would live if they could. (XIX, 250)

The real complexity of James's vision of life lies in the relationship between knowledge and action as these relate to the whole question of moral responsibility. Yet that question itself assumes alternative shapes in his imagination, with a kind of shadowy option suggested between real interior freedom and the mere illusion of it. Furthermore, though Milly's wilful blindness makes her one of the agents of the catastrophe, that catastrophe would have been inevitable even if she *hadn't* blinded herself to the facts. That is the terror of her position: she could not have avoided her doom by correctly seeing the situation around her. And again, what are our feelings at the end of the novel, when the disaster is an accomplished fact? Do we blame either Kate, the prime mover, for the results of practiced deception, or Milly for allowing herself to be practiced upon? *Merton* certainly blames Kate—in fact he goes to incredible lengths to see to what lengths she will go—but it is not at all clear that James does; besides, Merton has his own, rather unpalatable way of drawing ethical lines and splitting moral hairs.

On the other hand, the events of the novel do assert something about the outcome of certain forms of human behavior. All three of the protagonists are playing for the highest possible stakes: money, morality, love, life itself. And all three lose: their calculated risks collapse in a nightmare of death, dishonor, and distrust. What might be called Milly's suspension of disbelief betrays her just as certainly as Kate's and Merton's partnership in manipulation and deception betrays them. And these facts mean something.

It is possible, that is, to go through the novel and show that the principal agents are not responsible for what happens; it is also possible to show that they are. A paradoxical sense of things, antithetical modes of structuring and comprehending reality without granting authority to any one mode, is a fundamental characteristic of James's imagination. In many serious works of art, of course, one finds opposed assumptions about the nature and meaning of existence, assumptions whose value is expressive rather than explanatory. James, however, tends to systematize his structures, elaborate, juxtapose, and finally exhaust them. Without giving credence to any one—though each structure claims *for itself* absolute authority—he renders their inception, evolution, interplay, and destruction. The dreams of the characters are programs for existence, models to "better" reality. Each construct proposes itself to the character who fashions it as pre-emptive, inevitable, justifiable: a superior version of the conditions of life, designed for self-fulfillment. Only, the premises of the different models by definition exclude one another, and we are witnesses to the disintegration of the models that results when their conflicting premises are exposed.

On another level what we are given is the outcome, the end results, of certain forms of behavior, usually manipulation. The results are seen to destroy both those who practiced it and those upon whom it was practiced. James's tales in a way constitute cases in point from which it is possible to make certain inductions, usually about what will not work. We spoke earlier about his strange vision of the culpability of innocence as well as of knowledge. In relation to this matter, his novels are illustrations of the *practical* failure of both self-deception and the deception of others, and of the fact that the refusal to adjudicate between one's own needs and those of others simply does not work.

The question whether he sees greed and manipulation as *moral* failures is another matter altogether. In general, James utilizes moral constructs for the sake of the interest and intensity that result from their juxtaposition with other models for behavior. He is concerned with rendering the excruciation that results from exposing someone of a trusting, open, innocent nature to someone who, beneath a perfected social manner of grace and charm, hides deadly intents. Fascinated with his villains and with the general human capacity for destructiveness, he is often primarily involved in exploring the peripheral limits of that capacity in his characters. *The Awkward Age, What Maisie Knew,* and even the comparatively mild *Washington Square* are all, for example, studies of parental abuse of the young. As we saw in the first chapter, James has a tendency to be preoccupied with the process of victimization for its own sake, or for its sheer dramatic effect, by no means for its moral implications per se. In this sense, he has along with other American writers, an important kinship with Poe. D. H. Lawrence, in his *Studies in Classic American Literature,* recognizes a similar affinity between Poe and Hawthorne, and characterizes a tendency in American art that is at *least* as true of James (though Lawrence does not have a chapter on James) as it is of any of the writers the book deals with: "All the time there is this split in the American art and art-consciousness. On the top it is as nice as pie, goody-goody and lovey-dovey. Like Hawthorne being such a blue-eyed darling, in life, and Longfellow and the rest such sucking doves. . . .

"Serpents they were. Look at the inner meaning of their art and see what demons they were." [17]

The most obvious manifestations of this kind of duality in James are the studied contrasts between the manners and morals of America and Europe. Generally, James's treatment of manners has been much, if ambivalently, praised by critics, while his treatment of morals has

[17] (Garden City, New York, 1953), pp. 92–93.

caused dissatisfaction and been badly misinterpreted. He "knew . . . manners too well; he had penetrated too thoroughly," writes Leavis, who adds that it "is no doubt at first appearances odd that his interest in manners should have gone with such moral-intellectual intensity. But the manners he was interested in were to be the outward notation of spiritual and intellectual fineness, or at least to lend themselves to treatment as such. Essentially he was in quest of an ideal society." [18]

By "manners," Leavis means "the refinements of civilized intercourse" or "highly civilized" conduct. That of course is to narrow the possible meaning of the word from "a person's habitual behavior or conduct," or his "outward bearing" in general (to borrow one definition from *The American College Dictionary* and one from *The Oxford Universal Dictionary*), to a particular kind of behavior ("civilized"). The latter is a fair enough designation of one type of conduct James dealt with, but it certainly does not do justice to the range and complexity of his fascination with external behavior. In the broader sense of the term, the Pococks have "manners" too (though not refined ones) and ones that, however ironically, interest James greatly.

But a more important issue raised by Leavis is the nature of the relationship between a person's conduct in the world around him and his inner "self". According to Leavis, James intended a one-to-one correspondence between manners and morals, one's demeanor and one's "essence," one's mask and one's face. Sometimes this is the case: with Madame de Vionnet, pre-eminently. But by and large James's interest in manners is often exactly the

[18] *The Great Tradition*, p. 198.

opposite of the sort of equation Leavis posits. Most frequently, James's preoccupation lies with the profound *discrepancy* between the outward veneer of polish, wit, charm, "correctness," and the inward darkness of the human heart. Such a discrepancy is postulated for characters like Kate Croy, Madame Merle, Charlotte Stance, and the energy, interest—and horror—of the novels in which they appear are contingent upon it. Leavis has been beguiled too much by the goody-goody surface, the guise the serpent takes. The "outward notation" stands in deliberate ironic contrast to the inner spiritual reality and is intended as a disguise rather than a manifestation of the latter. Or the "manners" become a kind of muted, oblique language for concerns that lie far beneath their surface, regions of bliss and bale that have nothing to do with the drawing room:

He can convey an impression, an atmosphere of what you will with literally nothing. Embarrassment, chastened happiness— for his happiness is always tinged with regret—greed, horror, social vacuity—he can give you it all with a purely blank page. His characters will talk about rain, about the opera, about the moral aspects of the selling of Old Masters to the New Republic, and those conversations will convey to your mind that the quiet talkers are living in an atmosphere of horror, of bankruptcy, of passion hopeless as the Dies Iræ! . . . That, you know, is what life really is—a series of such meaningless episodes beneath the shadow of doom—or of impending bliss, if you prefer it. And that is what Henry James gives you—an immense body of work all dominated with that vibration— with that balancing of the mind between the great outlines and the petty details.[19]

[19] Ford Madox Hueffer, *Henry James: A Critical Study* (New York, 1916), pp. 153–155.

The Negative Imagination

It must be more clearly recognized that James's vision of human existence is first and last an ironic one, and that it is not he who is deceived by the glitter of the social façade he studies. He was in one sense in search of an ideal society, and the search took place in the two countries of his imagination that in effect constituted a mythological setting: America, the Pale Lady, the boring paradise, and Europe, the Dark Lady, seductive, sensual, totally attractive, totally wicked, the enchanting hell. His novels are all legends of the failure of the quest, because in *his* vision truth and beauty are not one. His Holy Grail is the golden bowl with the imperceptible flaw.

But the success of any ironic presentation depends first of all upon consistency of tone. Reuben Brower defines irony as "meaning . . . narrowed to opposition" and remarks that metaphor and irony "present two levels of meaning which the reader must entertain at once if he is to respond imaginatively to either of these forms of expression. . . . To experience the irony . . . we must entertain both of the clashing possibilities." [20] Even in works (the problem novels, for example) in which James deliberately renders reality from a multiplicity of perspectives, without giving authority to any one of them, each perspective is itself clear, and it is obvious that if either level of meaning (whether or not the clashing viewpoints are resolved ultimately) becomes obscured, or the author's attitude toward it is ambivalent or inconsistent,

[20] *The Fields of Light: An Experiment in Critical Reading* (New York, 1951), pp. 50–51. Brower adds, "So obvious a point needs stressing . . . because some definitions of irony imply that the reader finds the intended or true meaning beneath the apparent, a view that tends to destroy irony both as a literary experience and as a vision of life."

the ironic effect is lost in confusion. This is finally what happens with the figure of Merton Densher in *The Wings of the Dove*. Up to a point in the delineation of Densher, James's touch is sure and masterly as he keeps a fine and deliberate balance between Densher's increasingly distorted self-image and the more objective image of him held by others. Eugenio, for example, "took a view of him . . . essentially vulgar . . . the imputation in particular that, clever, *tanto bello* and not rich, the young man from London was—by the obvious way—pressing Miss Theale's fortune hard" (XX, 257). Densher's passivity, his self-deception and rationalization, his increasing helplessness and loss of freedom are superbly handled. One of the first consequences of his fall is the diminution in his power of "right reasoning": it is Kate's doing and not his. Or it is Milly's *and* his, freely, not Kate's at all; therefore he is not being manipulated, has not lost his manhood. His ethical position entails obedience to the law, not the spirit; action alone, and not intent or desire, is what is culpable. So long then as he doesn't *do* anything: tell a direct lie, propose marriage himself to Milly, he is blameless. The fact that he knows that both Kate and Aunt Maud have "told the proper lie" for him (that Kate doesn't love him) he passes over. And it will be all right if Milly proposes to him. He has, it is true, moments of clearer awareness, in which he wonders about the validity of his distinction between active and passive participation in the whole affair: "It was Kate's description of him, his defeated state, it was none of his own; his responsibility would begin, as he might say, only with acting it out. The sharp point was, however, in the difference between acting and not acting: this difference in fact it was that made the case of conscience. He saw it with a certain alarm rise before him that everything was acting that was not speaking the particular word" (that is, disabusing Milly of the notion that Kate is indifferent to him) (XX, 76).

He decides, however, that it would be "indelicate" to mention the matter to Milly when she would never dream of mentioning it to him, and that further there would be a kind of unnecessary "brutality" in shaking Milly off when she so clearly enjoys his company. At this point, he has not yet given Milly reason to believe that he has any kind of romantic interest in her, though that deception is imminent. The deception itself (what he calls "turning his corner") he perpetrates out of *politeness:* "Clearly what had occurred was her having wished it [that he accompany her on a drive] so that she had made him simply wish, in civil acknowledgement, to oblige *her*" (XX, 88). We are to take this extraordinary gesture at face value; he is quite sincere. It is extraordinary because, from here on out, he will not just disoblige but kill her if he does not keep up the pretense. This is the fateful moment, for *now* he would (so far as he knows) merely wound her feelings if he declines her invitation; *later* he would destroy her, as he himself quickly recognizes a few moments later: "If he might have turned tail . . . five minutes before, he could n't turn tail now" (XX, 90).

His politeness is a matter of real concern: he sees she yearns for him, he is touched by her "shy fragrance of heroism" (XX, 81). But his displacement of perspective is incredible, particularly in view of his awareness, en route to this very visit, that he was "the kind of man wise enough to mark the case in which chucking [someone] might be the minor evil and the least cruelty" (XX, 71). And so the code of chivalry becomes the Law that Merton obeys: "The single thing that was clear in complications was that, whatever happened, one was to behave as a gentleman. . . . The law was not to be a brute—in return for amiabilities" (XX, 183–184).

To be a blue-eyed darling in appearance and a serpent in fact—and not to recognize it. The irony of the portrait is intense, deliberate, and in splendid control until the concluding portions of the book, when something goes askew and the man who has tried so hard not to be a brute becomes what is almost worse, a prig. This was not James's intent of course: Merton was to have gone through a spiritual transformation—literally a conversion —to have conceived a "horror" of the scheme in which he had become involved, as James puts it in his notebooks, and to have emerged morally reborn, "faithful to the [exquisite] image of the dead." [21]

But a conversion implies a degree of self-examination and valuation (rejection of the sinful self) that never takes place in Merton.[22] He dreads public exposure and feels "a dire apprehension of publicity" (XX, 391), but this is about the limit of any self-scrutiny that we are shown. Because of this, his conversion is not persuasive, in the sense that we do not feel moved, convinced of some radical spiritual growth. It is one of those cases where

[21] *The Notebooks of Henry James,* ed. F. O. Matthiessen and Kenneth B. Murdock (New York, 1955), pp. 173–174.

[22] When Saul of Tarsus is on the road to Damascus and hears the voice of Christ saying "Saul, Saul, why persecutest thou me?" it is a private matter of conscience with respect to the implications in the stoning of Stephen. The behavior of the other Jews involved in the persecution is in no way relevant to his experience.

instead of being *shown*, as James would put it, we have to take the word of the "poor author" for it. About James's intention, there can be no question: the question is to what degree he realized it. He himself is the first to admit that sometimes an artist's plan is one thing, his result another. One reason we do not feel a sense of Densher's spiritual growth is that his concern is so little with himself, so exclusively and so harshly focused upon Kate. That he should feel a revulsion toward her is not, in itself, surprising, but the way in which he manifests it is very much unlike the "grace" Milly extended to him. He is nearly cruel. He sets little tests and traps for Kate like placing in her hands, to deal with at her option, both the letter from Milly and the envelope from her New York lawyers stating the amount she had left him. When Kate opens it—and who can conceive of her doing anything but—he confesses he is "disappointed": it wasn't the "handsome way" of renunciation he had hoped for; he had hoped she would return it unopened, accompanied by "an absolutely kind letter" (XX, 398) of refusal. When she points out that he neglected to express this hope in his letter to her, he explains, "I did n't want to. I wanted to leave it to yourself. I wanted—oh yes, if that's what you wish to ask me—to see what you'd do."

"You wanted to measure the possibilities of my departure from delicacy? . . ."

"Well, I wanted—in so good a case—to test you" (XX, 399). And test her he continues to do, up to the bitter end. "He had given poor Kate her freedom" (XX, 396), as he puts it: freedom to choose the money without him, or him without the money. So that once again she is in the very dilemma, caught between the same set of negative alternatives, that she was at the outset. There is nothing wrong with this degree of "poetic justice" descending on her shoulders, but there is something wrong with Merton's sanctimonious viciousness, especially when it is coupled with the comparatively gentle, forgiving attitude he has toward himself. He explains to Kate at one point that Sir Luke had understood that he had "meant awfully well"; at another, he senses that Mrs. Lowder gathered the "essence" of his situation: "The essence was that something had happened to him too beautiful and too sacred to describe. He had been, to his recovered sense, forgiven, dedicated, blessed" (XX, 343). But he does not extend to Kate the charity he, without tests, has received.

How then are we to understand these events with which the novel closes? Are we intended to make a split judgment, in which Merton is finally exonerated, but Kate not? If this is the intention, it certainly is not realized; in fact the emotional effect is just the opposite. There is a certain beauty in the brave if somewhat harrowing consistency of Kate's character, in her risking everything to gain everything. And this we feel right up through the end, in spite of Merton. Perhaps it is partly due to the principle cited by E. E. Stoll, that readers tend to identify with the active agent rather than the passive, whether that agent is morally acceptable to them or not.[23] At any rate, the bravery of her risk coupled with her refusal to rationalize her behavior, while most of Merton's energy is devoted to rationalization, helps to account for our greater sympathy for Kate. There is something much

[23] Elmer Edgar Stoll, "Give the Devil His Due," *Review of English Studies*, XX (April, 1944), 124.

more unpalatable about immorality when it is in the mask of piety than when it is frank and open.

I suspect that James's *scheme* for the novel, which we have in the notebooks, called for a kind of formal resolution of the plot that was incompatible with the profoundly paradoxical nature of his vision of the source and meaning of human suffering. It was mentioned earlier that much of the energy of the novel is logistical, rhetorical. James's concern with formal balance and opposition, and with fateful logic, is highly effective in the initial portions of the book, where it creates the feeling of impending catastrophe that is not to be eluded by any efforts on Milly's part. But James's preoccupation with the mathematics of situation badly weakens the ending. In a way, one could say that the two deepest artistic impulses—concern for shape, form, and aesthetic organization, and concern for truth—obtruded upon each other in this novel at its conclusion. Densher's actions and reactions toward Kate are both harsher and simpler than those of the total work, just as his reactions toward himself are kinder. But because this is the case, the novel can end "neatly," with Densher scarred but beautified and Kate plunged back into the original dilemma upon the altar of which she sacrificed her morality: Kate given and refusing one last option to renounce her lust for money; Kate not spiritually transformed as Densher supposedly is but in fact (that is in *effect*) is not. Kate is thus left formally, though once again this is not the emotional effect, bearing the brunt of the drama of pain that has been enacted. What the book makes so clear and the ending does not is that all three of the principal agents played their role in the events that took place, and that all three are at one and the same time responsible and not responsible. It is this ambivalent sense of things, constantly articulated throughout the book, that the ending does not, or cannot, rise to meet. The ending therefore undermines both the complexity and the emotional intensity of the work as a whole. Densher's sudden access to piety is accomplished with too much ease; he does not suffer enough in the sense that he escapes the self-confrontation that would be the symbolic recognition of and penance for some of the pangs Milly has endured at his hands. This in turn means that the whole moral order of events that centered around his figure has to be questioned: did James after all take him at his own valuation, as a reluctant pawn who is to be exonerated for having tried to be chivalrous in the middle of a compromising situation? And if James did take him that way, what then are we to make of the central ethical problem that is the really interesting and really powerful circumstance of Densher's position: that "case of conscience" which lay in the difference between acting and not acting on his part? If we accept the ending, we must dismiss the case of conscience as a mere rhetorical murmur to himself in the middle of the gentlemen's plight. Yet the book, fortunately, will not allow us to do that. In spite of the ending, Densher's passive involvement has implicated him deeply indeed. This at least is the effect, and it is a good thing that it is. If it were not, the whole novel would suffer from a superficiality, even sentimentality, of vision. But James explicitly consigned even to Milly responsibility for the outcome of events, and it is difficult to believe he did not intend at least the same burden of blame for Merton, if not quite a lot more. It does not seem convincing, that is, that James's intention was different from the effect created by the events of the novel up until the end. It is the ending that is un-persuasive, even unreal. The novel itself survives, but certainly at a cost to its integrity of effect and full realization of its own order of spiritual reality. In that order Merton *is* exonerated, but in a very different sense from that in which he exonerates himself, just as Kate is condemned on quite another level from that on which he condemns her: one considerably less legalistic, literal, and petty. He has of course applied the letter of the law to himself, earlier, so perhaps it is not surprising that he does so to Kate at the end. But the burden of the book rests upon violation not of the word but of the spirit. Is not the whole point that no "word" is spoken to Milly, that the crime and the woe are committed wordlessly but never-theless absolutely? It is this central human fact of the novel that the ending betrays, and it is in spite of the betrayal that the novel survives.

CHAPTER III

The Ambassadors

Like PARIS, the great "jewel" that is its setting, *The Ambassadors*[1] has a rare iridescence, luminosity of surface, and wealth of association. Though milder and more muted than *The Wings of the Dove* or *The Golden Bowl,* it is the most elaborate and richly textured of James's dramas of moral consciousness. It is unique too among the late works in its focus upon middle age (the "afternoon," the "twilight of life") rather than youth, for though the theme of youth is a predominant one in the book, our center of attention is a character far past that period in his life. In these respects—and perhaps in others—*The Ambassadors* has a certain spiritual kinship

[1] New York ed. (New York, 1909), XXI–XXII. Citations from *The Ambassadors* in my text are to this edition.

with *The Tempest*.[2] Like Prospero, Strether is exiled temporarily from his native ground into a place of enchantment:

In the garden of the Tuileries he had lingered, on two or three spots, to look; it was as if the wonderful Paris spring had stayed him as he roamed. The prompt Paris morning struck its cheerful notes—in a soft breeze and a sprinkled smell, in the light flit, over the garden-floor, of bareheaded girls. . . . The air had a taste as of something mixed with art, something that presented nature as a white-capped master-chef. (XXI, 79)

All three of the late novels make deliberate use of the fairy-tale mode: motifs of enchantment, spells, figurative or real princesses and princes, sorcerers, and fairy godmothers. But in none of the three is this mode used in so sustained and at the same time so quiet a way as in *The Ambassadors*, where it is an important yet unobtrusive element affecting the tone and texture of the entire novel. The air is "charged," "infectious": "Poor Strether had . . . to recognise the truth that wherever one paused in Paris the imagination reacted before one could stop it" (XXI, 96). And the texture woven by the imagination in this novel is elaborate, complex, and lustrous. "I dare say . . . , [remarks Maria] that I do, that we all do here, run too much to mere eye. But how can it be helped? We're all looking at each other—and in the light of Paris one sees what things resemble. That's what the light of

2 "In poetic drama—*The Tempest* (on which he wrote an essay), the plays of Racine, Maeterlinck, and Ibsen—James came nearest to finding precedents for his later novels. And in these plays are adumbrated the two devices which dominate one's recollection of the later James: close conversation and the metaphor." Austin Warren, *Rage for Order: Essays in Criticism* (Ann Arbor, Michigan, 1959), pp. 144–145.

Paris seems always to show. It's the fault of the light of Paris—dear old light!" (XXI, 207).

Part of the complexity, the richness of *The Ambassadors* is in fact directly due to the conscious utilization of the principle of "resemblance," the yoking together of heterogeneous associations and areas of experience through the unifying medium of Strether's consciousness. Everything that Strether sees is a kind of haunt, a presence that suggests or evokes the quality of another presence, usually one that is gone irretrievably, or even one that was never there but only yearned for. In England, his first taste of "Europe," he strolls and pauses "here and there for a dismantled gate or a bridged gap, with rises and drops, steps up and steps down, queer twists, queer contacts, peeps . . . under the brows of gables," and his reaction is one of intense pleasure coupled with immediate evocation of the past: "Too deep almost for words was the delight of these things to Strether; yet as deeply mixed with it were certain images of his inward picture. He had trod this walk in the far-off time, at twenty-five" (XXI, 15–16). And what in turn had been the feelings that accompanied him then, in his first and youthful sojourn: the need and yearning to utilize the experience as a creative foundation for his future life. This reaction "consecrated"—declared sacred—the significance of that early pilgrimage, and took the form of a "private pledge of his own to treat the occasion as a relation formed with the higher culture and see that, as they said at Woollett, it should bear a good harvest." But the pledge remained unfulfilled, so that the color of his *present* experience becomes a bleak sense of all "the promises to himself that he had after his other visit never kept" (XXI, 85), "mere sallow paint on the door of the temple of taste that he had dreamed of raising up" (XXI, 87).

This coupling of immediate, vivid sensory detail with the sense of the significance it might have had but didn't and now never can—of present unobtainable riches and past irrevocable bankruptcy—is the characteristic mode of perception in *The Ambassadors*. Strether defines it in himself as a tendency to "uncontrolled perceptions," by which he means not that his mind is a jungle watering-ground, but that his sense of personal privation is irrepressible and that he would be happier if it weren't. So he sits with Maria Gostrey in England at a small table with rose-colored shades on the lighted candles and recalls that he had been "to the theatre, even to the opera, in Boston, with Mrs. Newsome . . . but there had been no little confronted dinner, no pink lights, no whiff of vague sweetness, as a preliminary" (XXI, 50). Maria's dress, low at bosom and shoulders, and her throat circled with a broad red velvet band do not serve—directly—as an incentive to lust but rather as a "rueful" recollection that "Mrs. Newsome's dress was never in any degree 'cut down,' and she never wore round her throat a broad red velvet band." He then begins to think what that lady *did* wear (an Elizabethan ruche), conscious of his own mental processes yet helpless to control them. Every immediate impression of any intensity that Strether has, serves, like the red band, "as a starting-point for fresh backward, fresh forward, fresh lateral flights" (XXI, 51).

What Strether's consciousness both depicts and exemplifies here is the metaphoric imagination, the consistent presentation of which is largely responsible for the rich texture and thematic complexity of the novel. In addition, the statement the figures repeatedly make—"this is a symbol of all that I never had and never will"— determines the book's tone of bemused melancholy and passive yearning. We know that James wanted his protagonist to be *"fine,* clever, literary almost"[3] and that he considered but rejected making him a novelist (both on the grounds that that would be too much like William Dean Howells, whose impassioned plea to a mutual friend to "live" provided James the theme of *The Ambassadors,* and on the grounds that such a hero generally would be too improbable). James also rejected the possibility of making him an artist, because an artist, like a journalist, lawyer, or doctor "WOULD in a manner have 'lived.'"[4] But these considerations of a creative "type," though waived, are signficant, and his hero eventually was to be, in spite of his personal shortcomings and his failure to achieve an identity through work, a man of imagination.

And the paradox of his character—the man of imagination who is at the same time a New England puritan—is a central paradox, of which the European-American antithesis is but one symbolic projection. Strether, we are warned at the outset, is burdened "with the oddity of a double consciousness. There was detachment in his zeal and curiosity in his indifference" (XXI, 5). In the immediate context, this refers to his ambivalence at the prospect of meeting Waymarsh, whose presence he wishes for yet whose absence he enjoys "extremely." But the

---

[3] *The Notebooks of Henry James,* ed. F. O. Matthiessen and Kenneth B. Murdock (New York, 1955), p. 226.

[4] *Ibid.,* p. 227.

broader context is the significance this meeting has for Strether, for Waymarsh is the true American representative, who is second only to the unseen yet ubiquitous Mrs. Newsome. He is an original specimen of the most typical New World genus: "a truly majestic aboriginal," the Great Father, the "American statesman . . . trained in 'Congressional halls,' of an elder day" (XXI, 25). The delay in their meeting means for Strether "such a consciousness of personal freedom as he had n't known for years," freedom to give over "his afternoon and evening to the immediate and the sensible" (XXI, 4).

It is of course because Waymarsh is the externalization of one of Strether's inward voices that he dreads meeting him. If Strether did not have susceptibilities of conscience against his own delight in the "immediate and the sensible," he would feel no alarm. Not only does he have them, however, but they increase in intensity with the amount of pleasure he feels, so that strolling in the early morning of Paris, which hangs before him "the vast bright Babylon, like some huge iridescent object, a jewel brilliant and hard . . . twinkled and trembled and melted together . . . all surface one moment . . . all depth the next" (XXI, 89), he is tormented with a kind of moral uneasiness. It takes the form of a rhetorical problem: "Was it at all possible . . . to like Paris enough without liking it too much?" (XXI, 90). The implicit accusation of course is that *any* liking is, by definition, "too much"—and Strether does like it.

This war between the sense of rectitude and the sense of beauty is the basic conflict of the novel, as it is the basic conflict of Strether's character; indeed the former is simply an extension or elaboration of the latter. The book is not about Europe and America, or even about Europeans and Americans. It is about the significance that each place and its inhabitants have for a man burdened with "a double consciousness." What we are given is a complex study not in twofold but in fourfold reactions, for Strether is ambivalent to *both* of the great civilizations that are the symbolic terrain of his own internal struggle. It is by no means just Europe to which his responses are divided, though that continent is the actual setting of the events of the novel and is indeed Babylon to his feelings: place of iniquity, home of whores, yet precious beyond words, a temple, like Maria Gostrey's nest, to "the lust of the eyes and the pride of life" (XXI, 119).

Though James typically is concerned with the *relation* of consciousness to the external human scene, finding in aspects of the latter analogues for the former (or items of special significance to it), the nature of that scene becomes progressively more abstract in each of the last three novels until, in *The Golden Bowl,* the external world has receded as an "interesting" tactile and visual field (with a few exceptions such as the scene of the purchase of the bowl in the shop). The source of particularity, the texture of sensuous surfaces in that novel, comes instead primarily from the luminous, elaborate metaphors by means of which the characters through whose eyes the story is seen objectify their perceptions. That work also achieves particularity by means of tableaux in which the choreography of the principal characters—physical movements of slow pursuit along a terrace, "significant" regroupings around a table, and so forth—are at one and the same time symbolic of various games of manipulation and deceit being played among them and the literal means by which the "play" becomes actuality and the deceit (or whatever) accomplished, ratified. Such scenes are "vivid," theatrical, and in them the outer world does figure, but rather more in the manner of a stage setting, a backdrop, than as a projection of three-dimensional external reality in which the characters are continuously "located."

In *The Ambassadors* (completed before but published after *The Wings of the Dove*), however, the "setting"—though as we have indicated it stands in analogic relation to conflicting aspects of Strether's consciousness—*is* projected in its three-dimensionality and detailed concreteness. The drama of the hero's sensibility takes place in a context of intensely vivid social realities—attitudes, customs, modes of thought and behavior, American speech and dress, Parisian gardens, streets, interior landscapes—which have *both* an extrinsic and an intrinsic relation to that sensibility.

In the novel we are given an extended ironic characterization of middle-class American and upper-class Parisian culture, "a comic work" as it has been observed, "in the general tradition of Molière and Jane Austen." [5] At the same time, however, its scope is far broader, its range of tone more complex than the typical "novel of manners." The effectiveness of Jane Austen's work, for example, largely depends upon the unquestioned acceptance of a fixed social and ethical code of behavior, deviations from which can be examined with minute

[5] Richard Chase, "James' *Ambassadors*," *Twelve Original Essays on Great American Novels*, ed. Charles Shapiro (Detroit, 1958), p. 129.

exactness. But *The Ambassadors* has for its framework not one but two such codes, in radical opposition, neither of which in the final analysis completely triumphs or is completely defeated. It is in the study of half-victories and partial defeats of two world views as they relate to the personal history of Lambert Strether that the significance of the novel lies, for whatever its context, it is first and last his story. The lives of the other characters, as well as the cultural settings in which they take place, have meaning for us only as they have meaning for Strether, whose feelings, responses, perceptions, and reactions constitute the subject matter of the book.

So that the pertinent question is the nature of the relationship between the European-American dichotomy in the novel and the private life of Lambert Strether, the "ambassador" on a temporary mission from Woollett, Massachusetts, to Paris, France. The nature of his mission, as we know, is to fetch back to the bosom of his home, family, and "business" young Chad Newsome, whose protracted stay in Paris, it is believed in Woollett, means that he is in the clutches of an immoral woman. What actually happens in the book is in a sense relatively simple: Strether undergoes two major shifts in his attitude toward his mission. Initially he is fully primed with the Woollett concept—that the female in question, whoever she is, is not "even an apology for a decent woman" (XXII, 202)—and considers it of the greatest importance that Chad at once break with everything and return straight home. The first shift comes after he encounters both Chad, who has changed in manner and appearance from a condition of relative mediocrity to one of relative magnificence, and Madame de Vionnet, who, a little to his disappointment, has nothing about her of the tart he had expected. Impressed by Chad, charmed by Madame de Vionnet, Strether comes to the conclusion, in which he is abetted by overt statements from both Chad himself and the latter's friend little Bilham, that the attachment between the couple is a "virtuous" one and that Chad must therefore not desert her. The second shift comes when he discovers after a chance meeting with the couple in the French countryside that their attachment is *not* "virtuous," that it is sexual, and that he has been deceived. But by then, sick and disillusioned though he is—"It was the quantity of make-believe involved and so vividly exemplified that most disagreed with his spiritual stomach" (XXII, 265)—something of major significance has happened to Strether's concept of "virtue." His final stance is that even though the affair is not only sexual but adulterous, Chad would be "a criminal of the deepest dye" (XXII, 311) to abandon a woman who has aided him so, who has sacrificed so much for him, and who loves him so. "You owe her everything," he tells Chad at the end, "very much more than she can ever owe you. You've in other words duties to her, of the most positive sort; and I don't see what other duties—as the others are presented to you—can be held to go before them" (XXII, 313).

This essentially is the plot of the novel, and upon those two simple shifts in Strether's attitude hangs a tale half comic, half tragic, certainly pathetic, of the struggle of a complex and somewhat befuddled psyche to find, before it is too late, some meaning, significance, and beauty in life. One might say that the book is about how he almost finds it: almost, but not quite.

Europe and America each offers to Strether its own

modus vivendi, its own elaborately articulated set of possibilities and philosophy of existence. That the basic assumptions of each are violently antithetical is something that Strether at first accepts as a matter of course, then in his hopeful delusion about "virtuous attachments" discards, then comes again painfully to recognize. But by that time a strange and complex interaction of the two styles of life has taken place within Strether, with the result that each has operated upon the other with something of the effect of a slow poison. He is left in the end with a lingering distaste—coupled with a nostalgia for the beauty that was almost truth too—for both places, a permanent spiritual exile, in possession only of the rather pathetic consolation that he had "not, out of the whole affair" (XXII, 326), got anything for himself and has therefore, in some obscure but honorable way, been "right."

The great values upheld and cherished by Woollett are conformity, which passes as "equality," and rectitude. There are but two "types" in Woollett, the male and the female, and on any subject whatsoever but "two or three" opinions. One of Strether's first impressions of Europe is his sense of the multifold discriminations, rankings, and categories that, by contrast, are indulged in there. Miss Gostrey, he recognizes, was "the mistress of a hundred cases or categories, receptacles of the mind, subdivisions for convenience, in which, from a full experience, she pigeon-holed her fellow mortals with a hand as free as that of a compositor scattering type. She was as equipped in this particular as Strether was the reverse" (XXI, 11). This concept of "personal types" becomes the keynote of Europe for Strether, part of whose growth of experience consists in his increasing ability to recognize them when he sees them. But the significant thing is the concept itself, the very notion of a hierarchical ordering of values, rather than the degree of skill he shows in its practical application. It is a concept regarded with the profoundest mistrust and abhorrence by the sister communities and companions-at-arms, Milrose, Connecticut, and Woollett, Massachusetts, for it reeks of political and spiritual decadence, the old order, and the old, castoff world. Its great emblem is the Catholic Church: "The Catholic Church, for Waymarsh—that was to say the enemy, the monster of bulging eyes and far-reaching quivering groping tentacles—was exactly society, exactly the multiplication of shibboleths, exactly the discrimination of types and tones, exactly the wicked old Rows of Chester, rank with feudalism; exactly in short Europe" (XXI, 41).

But what does it mean for the errant Strether? The chain of his association that leads to this perception of what Europe means to Waymarsh is significant here. The two of them, with Miss Gostrey, are strolling and gazing into shop windows, Waymarsh maintaining "an ambiguous dumbness that might have represented either the growth of a perception or the despair of one" (XXI, 39) and looking "guilty and furtive" when his eye happens to be caught by some object of minor interest. Strether, however, is utterly entranced and apologizes for his rapture on the grounds of previous deprivation: "Do what he might . . . his previous virtue was still there, and it seemed fairly to stare at him out of the windows of shops that were not as the shops of Woollett, fairly to make him want things that he should n't know what to do with. It

was by the oddest, the least admissible of laws demoralis-
ing him now; and the way it boldly took was to make him
want more wants" (XXI, 40). He and Miss Gostrey find
themselves disposed to talk as "society" talks, and discuss
clothing, passers-by, faces, types: "Was what was happening to himself then . . . really that a woman of fashion
was floating him into society and that an old friend
deserted on the brink was watching the force of the
current?" She allows him to buy a pair of gloves, and it is
then that he realizes that for Waymarsh "mere discriminations about a pair of gloves" is emblematic of the
fundamental wantonness of Europe and that Strether for
indulging in such discriminations is like a "Jesuit in
petticoats, a representative of the recruiting interests of
the Catholic Church" (XXI, 41).

What we have here is a complex set of associations and
significances, all stemming from the single concept of
"type," and having implications of a very broad range
indeed. One of the most pertinent of these implications is
the connection between that aspect of experience involving the making of "discriminations" and the phenomenon
of taste. For a hierarchical ordering of values is a
necessary condition of the latter: without it a sense of
what is fitting, harmonious, or beautiful is impossible.
That Strether applies it at the moment to a pair of gloves
instead of, say, a painting is beside the point. What
matters is the phenomenon itself: it is one of the
possibilities of life that Europe offers and that America
denies him.

Closely connected to the notion of taste—indeed an
intricate part of it—is the whole realm of fluid, sensuous
experience, of "sensible impressions and agreeable sensa-

tions," of strolls "where the low-browed galleries were darkest, the opposite gables queerest, the solicitations of every kind densest" (XXI, 39). It was the delight of such that was "too deep almost for words" (XXI, 16) for Strether as he wandered earlier with Miss Gostrey, just as it is Waymarsh's present source of guilt and furtiveness when in spite of himself his eye happens to linger upon some interesting object. But if Strether's reaction had been merely delight, we would have a different novel; in fact, he shares with his fellow New Englander the pain of a stricken conscience, the inability wholly to give himself over to the flux of immediate experience. With Miss Gostrey he feels "as if this were wrong"; he labels the feeling "the terror. . . . I'm always considering something else; something else, I mean, than the thing of the moment. The obsession of the other thing is the terror" (XXI, 19). At the same time, he longs "unspeakably" to escape the obsession, goes so far as to beg her to help him do so.

Now this "failure to enjoy" is a "general" failure (XXI, 16), as Strether tells Maria: it is not a personal flaw in either himself or Waymarsh, but rather an habitual trait of the New England conscience whose responses are dictated by the moral imperatives of "ought" and "ought not" (Woollett "isn't sure it ought to enjoy. If it were it would"). Woollett of course is in no such state of uncertainty as Strether pretends with respect to the lust of the eyes. Woollett is perfectly sure it ought not to enjoy: after all it is the New Testament, not the Old, that requests us to pluck out our right eye if it offends us. The direct Biblical connection is with the sin of adultery, as it is reinterpreted by Christ to involve desire as well as action: "But I say unto you, That whosoever looketh on a woman to lust after her hath committed adultery with her already in his heart" (*Matthew* V, 28). But the Sermon on the Mount mentions the eye in another connection too: with respect to its yearning for mammon and the treasures of the earth, which "moths and rust doth corrupt." The use of wealth specifically for food, drink, and clothing is condemned: "And why take ye thought for raiment? Consider the lilies of the field. . . . Even Solomon in all his glory was not arrayed like one of these." Poor Strether and his pair of gloves; no wonder he is painfully aware that Waymarsh considers him not only "sophisticated" and "worldly" but also "wicked," the three indeed being, to the New England conscience, synonymous. Later this is made explicit as it comes to Strether "somehow to and fro that what poor Waymarsh meant was 'I told you so—that you'd lose your immortal soul!'" (XXI, 172–173).

So one of the dilemmas Strether is in as a man of taste burdened with puritan leanings is that the very things which most gratify his sensibility are the ones which most distress his conscience. Though he does not think (except ironically) in orthodox theological terms, he has internalized the trappings of Protestantism to the extent that his consciousness of the agreeable is continually marred by his consciousness of sin. Hence, he never has an unambiguous reaction to the delights of Paris: making a "frantic friend" (XXI, 120) of little Bilham, finding himself moved and pleased by, if not envious of, the latter's tranquillity, he still thinks: "It was by little Bilham's amazing serenity that he had at first been affected, but he had inevitably, in his circumspection, felt it as the trail of the serpent, the corruption, as he might conveniently have said, of Europe" (XXI, 125). At the same time, Paris continually seduces him: it makes him "want more wants," it gives him a taste of "personal freedom" (XXI, 4) such as he has not known for years, accompanied by "the full sweetness of the taste of leisure" (XXI, 39), fills him with "that apprehension of the interesting" (XXI, 49) totally unavailable in Woollett, Massachusetts, offers to him the "delicate and appetising" (XXI, 94) effects of tone and tint. The effect of this split response is that as his exposure to Paris deepens, both sides of his conflict intensify. The purity, the rectitude, the reliability of the American character become something he yearns more and more to find in its European counterpart, while the flatness, the Philistinism, the inflexibility of the former grow increasingly distasteful to him, just as his suspicion of the Parisian serpent enlarges as its seductive powers more and more envelop him. He is becoming at one and the same time more alienated from and more involved with both civilizations.

The focus of this conflict is the relationship between Chad and Madame de Vionnet and the nature of Strether's own role with respect to it. Whatever his other inward inconsistencies, Strether is consistent in always living by his sense of duty. In the beginning, this sense is identical with Woollett's, but what happens in the book is a great swing from a public to a private conscience, from an established, predetermined, black-and-white, fixed code of conduct to a personal, flexible, more relativist code in which each case is judged by its own merits. This shift is foreshadowed early in the novel, in a conversation with Maria:

"You've accepted the mission of separating him from the wicked woman. Are you quite sure she's very bad for him?"

Something in his manner showed it as quite pulling him up. "Of course we are. Wouldn't *you* be?"

"Oh, I don't know. One never does—does one?—beforehand. One can only judge on the facts. Yours are quite new to me." (XXI, 54)

Madame de Vionnet's "case" in Woollett's eyes is precisely that of a violator of a general code. Woollett's reasoning is syllogistic, deductive: all fornicators (they don't yet know that she is an adulteress) are immoral, Madame de Vionnet is a fornicator, therefore she is immoral. Strether, confronted with the example in the flesh and also by this time deeply involved in his own conflicting responses to Europe, is forced to re-examine his premises and ultimately to reason inductively. But it happens in a queer, roundabout way: in his attempt to reconcile the irreconcilable, he denies the *second* premise, not the first, until the bitter end. In so doing, he is able for a while to cling to the ethical system (absolute right and wrong, which are knowable) upon which he was reared, and thus to find the goodness that is America in the very heart of the charm that is Europe. What is at stake is considerably more than the possibility of an error of judgment about the nature of a given relationship: it is a whole way of life, an entire system of thought, belief, and behavior, a set of assumptions about the nature and significance of existence. He abandons the assumption of absolute right and wrong only when he is forced to, and comes finally to equate "virtue" with concepts other than celibacy; but it is a private equation he arrives at, a lonely one, one that Woollett would never accept in a thousand years. Madame de Vionnet always remains charming to him, but her virtue does not consist in her charm (at least not to his moral, though admittedly to his aesthetic, sense). It consists rather in her personal sacrifice to Chad: the devotion and love she has poured on him, the assistance she has rendered him, the man she has more or less made out of unpromising raw materials. It is not that Woollett would not recognize these as desirable attributes in a wife; but in a mistress they are merely further symptoms of wantonness.

Strether's personal moral history with respect to his attitude toward Madame de Vionnet is a re-enactment of a change in American cultural patterns that took place in the nineteenth century; the breakdown of the old puritanical code of conscience and the establishment of a new, freer, more relativistic code. The change in each case was for much the same reason: the old canon did not fit all situations, was too harsh, tended to ignore human considerations and distort the truth. So James writes, "*The false position, for our belated man of the world . . . was obviously to have presented himself at the gate of that boundless menagerie primed with a moral scheme of the most approved pattern which was yet framed to break down on any approach to vivid facts; that is to any at all liberal appreciation of them.*" [6]

What then is the difference between Strether and Chad, whose moral transportations may be said to be similar, at least up to a point? The difference is significant in its

[6] *The Art of the Novel: Critical Prefaces*, ed. R. P. Blackmur (New York, 1962), p. 315.

intuition of two divergent trends in American culture, both of which are connected with the breakdown of the puritan standard of ethics. Chad's relativism leads him directly into opportunism, manipulation, and exploitation: it is he who is the advertising man of the future. Strether's relativism on the other hand leads him to a struggle for a code of honor outside any system, to some private ideal of selflessness and personal allegiance, the significance of human ties, of intimacy, passion, and pain. The New England conscience had its strengths as well as its weaknesses, and one of its strengths was the sanctioning of the idea of behavior based upon responsibility toward one's fellows. This Strether preserves all the way through, though its form, significance, and finality have altered for him by the time the events have run their course.

But there are other differences between Strether and Chad too, not the least of which is that Chad is "the young man marked out by women" (XXI, 153). Once again, Strether's associations in connection with this perception are pertinent, as they link different areas of experience that together form part of the significance of his European adventure. Chad, he recognizes in their first conversation, not only is handsomer than he remembers him, but also is completely made over. His manners are "formed," he is a gentleman and man of the world, in other words "a man to whom things had happened and were variously known" (XXI, 152). Like a work of art, he has "a form and a surface," a design, tone, accent. His "identity so rounded off" and his "massive young manhood" hint at "some self-respect." It occurs then to Strether that the proper designation for this young man marked out by women is that of an "irreducible young

Pagan." The qualities of Chad's Parisian sea change thus are sophistication, worldliness, taste, youth, and potency: a sensuous, polished surface and a sexual, pagan nature.

And in spite of Strether's sense of duty, his insistence that the only way he can be "right" is to get nothing out of the whole affair for himself, he does have a personal investment in the lives of Chad Newsome and Madame de Vionnet. They represent for him his last chance to "live," through vicarious participation in their experiences. His capitulation to and defense of them (and therefore, by extension, of Europe) is, he confesses to Maria, his "surrender," his "tribute" to youth: "It has to come in somewhere, if only out of the lives, the conditions, the feelings of other persons. . . . The point is that they're mine. Yes, they're my youth; since somehow at the right time nothing else ever was" (XXII, 51).

Strether thus joins the long list of characters in James, those who achieve their strongest emotional satisfactions by observing and sometimes manipulating the lives of others: the Olive Chancellors, Susan Stringhams, Fanny Assinghams, and Ralph Touchetts. The type reaches its apotheosis in *The Portrait of a Lady*, in the figure of Gilbert Osmond, who literally cannot survive without a host, in vacuum, and whose whole identity is determined by the opinion of that shifting and nebulous personality known as "society." ("I *am* convention," he tells Isabel at one point.) And certainly Strether partakes of the characteristics of this type, though he is a very different breed of it from Osmond. Like Osmond, however, he has no coherent inward sense of himself ("He was Lambert Strether because he was on the cover, whereas it should have been, for anything like glory, that he was on the cover because he was Lambert Strether") (XXI, 84); like

Ralph, in his twilight hours he makes a bid for a degree of personal pleasure by vicariously investing his feeling. Strether's rationale for the attempt is not unlike Ralph's either: it is "too late" for him to act on his own behalf: the most he can do is to act on and through others, in an oblique attempt to find the youth he himself never had.

The Ambassadors has been objected to precisely on the grounds of Strether's passivity and the vicarious quality of his experience, with critics remarking that these attributes are responsible for a certain attenuated quality about the novel that persists in spite of its obvious charm. Richard Chase writes that the "general lack of masculine reciprocation, especially in Strether himself, accounts in part for the somewhat tenuous quality—the softness at the center—of life as depicted in James' novel . . . despite the wealth of reported observation," [7] and then goes on to compare (a comparison he acknowledges is invidious) the novel unfavorably with *Antony and Cleopatra*. And Matthiessen writes,

The burden of *The Ambassadors* is that Strether has awakened to a wholly new sense of life. Yet he does nothing at all to fulfill that sense. Therefore, fond as James is of him, we cannot help feeling his relative emptiness. At times, even . . . it is forced upon us that, despite James' humorous awareness of the inadequacy of his hero's adventures, neither Strether nor his creator escape a certain soft fussiness.[8]

Such remarks come down to a moral—not aesthetic—demand that a novelist conceive of his characters in terms of the most dubious banalities: unexamined cultural

[7] *Twelve Original Essays,* p. 136.
[8] *Henry James: The Major Phase* (New York, 1944), p. 39.

stereotypes having to do with "masculinity," aggres-
siveness, and so forth. Behind this in turn lies a conception of art based on standards lifted without ex-
amination from realistic fiction: art should directly
engage and passionately move the spectator by its imitation of the texture of daily life, its representation of
"real" (in this case sexually vigorous) three-dimensional
people.

James himself of course repeatedly insists upon the
intimate connection between art and life. In the Preface
to *The Portrait of a Lady*, he emphasizes "the perfect
dependence of the 'moral' sense of a work of art on the
amount of felt life concerned in producing it" [9] and in the
Preface to *The Ambassadors*, he writes, "Art deals with
what we see, it must first contribute full-handed that
ingredient; it plucks its material . . . in the garden of
life—which material elsewhere grown is stale and
uneatable." [10] But the amount of "felt life" evoked comes
down ultimately to "the artist's prime sensibility," the
"quality and capacity" of which represent the work's
"projected morality." This attribute itself is finally viewed
by James as "some mark made on the intelligence." In
other words, the measure of "life" in a work of art for
James turns out to be the intensity and complexity of the
consciousness that is operating upon the material it
receives from the external world. From this vantage point,
notions like "masculine reciprocity" are not only irrelevant but needlessly confusing: they tell us nothing about
James's art for better or for worse, and ask us to bring to
bear upon that art standards that obscure, not clarify, its
nature.

[9] *The Art of the Novel*, p. 45.   [10] *Ibid.*, p. 312.

In the case of Strether, James determined to make his a drama of consciousness rather than of action in part because of

the dreadful little old tradition, one of the platitudes of the human comedy, that people's moral scheme *does* break down in Paris. . . . [and to avoid the platitude James decided] The revolution performed by Strether under the influence of the most interesting of great cities was to have nothing to do with any *bêtise* of the imputably "tempted" state; he was to be thrown forward, rather, thrown quite with violence, upon his lifelong trick of intense reflexion.[11]

Moreover, while it is true enough in a sense that "the burden" of the novel is that its hero "has awakened to a wholly new sense of life," the fact that he does not fulfill himself is not a lapse on James's part but is, on the contrary, deliberate. Speaking of Strether's cry to little Bilham to "live"—which is both the "germ" of the novel and an "independent particle" lurking "in [its] mass"—[12] James writes,

He has accordingly missed too much, though perhaps after all constitutionally qualified for a much better part, and he wakes up to it in conditions that press the spring of a terrible question. *Would* there yet perhaps be time for reparation?—reparation, that is, for the injury done his character; for the affront, he is quite ready to say, so stupidly put upon it and in which he has even himself had so clumsy a hand? The answer to which is that he now at all events *sees;* so that the business of my tale and the march of my action, not to say the precious moral of everything, is just my demonstration of this process of vision.[13]

---

[11] *Ibid.*, p. 316.   [12] *Ibid.*, p. 307.   [13] *Ibid.*, p. 308.

James answers obliquely the question whether Strether would have enough time to make up for all he has missed, and the answer is negative: there isn't enough time, but at least Strether sees—what he has missed and that it is too late for reparation. Like his creator, he "was to go without many things, ever so many—as all persons do in whom contemplation takes so much the place of action." [14] The excruciation of the novel, its intensity, is precisely *due to* the contrast between Strether's awakened sense of what might have been and what is—or, to put it another way, his awareness that what might have been and what can never be are one and the same. The blow to him is total: the past is undone, the future without promise, the present both a reminder and a measure of both.

Matthiessen comes much closer to an objective and sensitive view of James's art and its relation to life earlier in his study when he writes, apropos of James's fascination with "seeing" and spectatorship in general, that this "was to mean that of the two types into which Yeats divides artists, those who, like Blake, celebrate their own immediate share in the energy that 'is eternal delight,' and those who, like Keats, give us a poignant sense of being separated from what they present, James belonged to the latter." [15]

It is true that James himself was much preoccupied with the whole matter of the definition of experience, in particular its dialectical relation to the dichotomy between action and contemplation. Furthermore, the pre-

[14] Henry James, *Autobiography: A Small Boy and Others; Notes of a Son and Brother; The Middle Years,* ed. F. W. Dupee (New York, 1956), p. 17.

[15] *Henry James,* p. 31.

occupation was a highly personal one. In this sense, Strether does embody some quintessential aspect of his author. The former is to learn retrospectively what James suggests his elders sensed prospectively about him when he was a child. Speaking of his freedom to wander, to "dawdle and gape," he writes, "what I look back to as my infant license can only have had for its ground some timely conviction on the part of my elders that the only form of riot or revel ever known to me would be that of the visiting mind." [16] In this same passage James, while speaking ruefully and compassionately of this "fore-doomed" figure of himself as a small boy rubbing his "contemplative nose" against iron rails, nevertheless manages to transform that objective pauper into a subjective prince, an aristocrat of sensibility and the responding consciousness:

He [the boy] might well have been even happier than he was. For there was the very pattern and measure of all he was to demand: just to *be* somewhere—almost anywhere would do—and somehow receive an impression or an accession, feel a relation or a vibration. . . . What it all appreciably gave him . . . [was] an education like another: feeling, as he has come to do more and more, that no education avails for the intelligence that doesn't stir some subjective passion, and that on the other hand almost anything that does so act is largely educative.[17]

The notion that the wealth of response and the sense of personal deprivation are somehow a function of each other is a continuous motif in James's work. In Strether's case, for example, things (such as Maria Gostrey's red velvet throat band) become precious and are in fact

[16] *Autobiography*, p. 16.   [17] *Ibid.*, p. 17.

noticed to begin with because they symbolize [18] all that he has ever yearned for and what he can never have. To have "lived" for Strether would have been to be in some state of possession in relation to the objects that pass before his eye: objects noticed by him in the first place because they stir his senses and because of their suggestibility. The human mind is, for James, by definition a haunted mind.

The haunting, furthermore, was implicit for him in the nature of consciousness, as the mode by which we both encounter life and are detached from it. For James, "experience" had two meanings, which themselves stand in an analogical relation to this opposition in the make-up of consciousness. On the one hand, experience meant action: the effective imposition of one's will upon the external world,[19] participation, mastery; on the other, it meant *re*action, a response of the mind, "a mark made on the intelligence," contemplation, passivity.

The first was something James could not imagine for himself. One of his earliest impressions, as we have seen,

[18] By "symbol" I mean an infinitely suggestible concretization provoking (perhaps "inciting") further concretizations.

[19] "Would," said Ortega y Gasset, "that our lives did take place inside ourselves! Then life would be the easiest thing imaginable: it would be to float in its own element. But life is as far as possible from a subjective phenomenon. It is the most objective of all realities. It is a man's *I* finding itself submerged in precisely what is not himself, in the pure *other* which is his environment. To live is to be outside oneself, to realize oneself.—The vital program which each one of us irremediably is, overpowers environment to lodge itself there. This unity of dramatic dynamism between the two elements, the I and the world—is life." *The Dehumanization of Art and Other Writings on Art and Culture* (Garden City, New York, 1956), p. 131.

was that for him these two ways of being in the world were mutually exclusive. By a feat of intelligence that did not quite satisfy his yearning to be "other" than he was (other than contemplative), he transformed the latter definition into the one delineating the superior mode of being. Finally, experience wasn't experience unless it stirred that "vibration" and anything that did so—a mere act of seeing—qualified. But the other notion lingered in his imagination. One of the consequences of this was his art itself, in particular its central preoccupations, which are with the nature of consciousness as the "vibrating" recipient of impressions from the external world; its method, which is the imitation of precisely that process; and its forms, which are analogues for the capacity of the responding mind to shape its impressions, to create an architecture for them.

His characters repeat the process their author engages in: they construct imaginary worlds with their "visiting" minds, worlds that are the objectification of their desires but that are also unreal and doomed to collapse when brought into conjunction with the "facts." The facts are always that things are different from what a given character had wanted. The basic pattern of James's work is the creation and collapse of the fiction, its failure.

On another level, his sense of separation from life in its more energetic forms reflects itself in a continual yearning not for reality but for a kind of Marvellian paradise where peaches thrust themselves into his hands. He pines, that is, for an impossible and idyllic kind of gratification, yet when he reaches out in hunger he tastes only ashes. Between these two extremes he is characteristically unable to find peace. We have remarked earlier upon the essential ambivalence that lies at the center of his vision of life, and upon its typical embodiment in a dramatic situation that takes the form of a dilemma in which the actor is faced with a choice—but a choice that he tries not to make—between equally desirable goods on the one hand and equally undesirable ills on the other. Kate Croy, Milly Theale, and Maggie Verver all reject the premise that they must choose between one good and another: they try for everything. Milly looks down from the cliff, and Susan Stringham watching her wonders rhetorically if she is choosing among the kingdoms of the earth or if she wants them all. Kate, as we have seen, refuses to have Densher without a fortune or a fortune without Densher. And Maggie Verver tries to hold her husband to one breast and her father to the other. Strether, too, refuses to choose or to make a compromise between the set of possibilities represented by Europe and the set represented by America. Very much like Milly, through the process of self-deception, he at first clings to the belief that he can have the best (and none of the worst) of both worlds; then, undeluded, he renounces both. Strether, too, turns his face to the wall.

Nobody in James, hero or villain, ever gets what he wants. Or, if by some chance he gets what he thinks he wants, it has turned to poison. So Kate gets her fortune but finds that because of it she has lost her man. So Maggie keeps her husband but finds that she cannot look into his eyes because of the dread of seeing in them what she has done: to him, to Charlotte, to her father, to herself. In spite of the greed, the hunger, the so-obvious yearning for gratification that characterize the Jamesian actor, the inevitable outcome of events is frustration, pain, loss. James, concerned as he is with the destruction and collapse of the fiction, has essentially a negative rather than a tragic imagination.

In spite of his fundamental affinities with Hawthorne, he is in this respect closer to Poe, just as he is closer to Joyce and the early Eliot than to Lawrence, Faulkner, or Hemingway. Each of the latter has some version of a positive vision, a dialectic of salvation: Hemingway's ethos of the bull ring and rules of the game; Lawrence's prototype of blood and lust; Faulkner's process of sacrificial expiation and his celebration of the virtue of endurance. James has no such vision, nothing even remotely resembling it. Like Joyce, he portrays a pervasive emotional and spiritual paralysis, but he does not share Joyce's avowed visionary moral purpose in so doing. James's interest is in drama, not in persuasion.

This must be granted him. There exists no aesthetic basis for insisting that a writer feel and write "positively," or with tragic grandeur. We should grant the writer his donnée, as James said. From that point on what we can do is make the effort to articulate, with reasonable dispassion, the nature and various literary effects of the artist's symbolic world and the manner in which it is presented.

One of the main traits of James's symbolic world is indirection: of thought, speech, behavior, and feeling. It manifests itself in part in the persistent, almost ritualistic use of social masks and deceptive appearances, upon the uncovering of which so much of his ironic effect depends. Typically, the closest "friend" (Madame Merle, Kate Croy), unmasked, is the deadliest enemy; the "faithful" husband or lover in fact deeply attached to someone else;

the affectionate mother (Mrs. Brooks, Charlotte Verver)
the most ruthless sexual rival. In these kinds of oppositions and reversals, and in the starkness of the conflict, the
agony of betrayal so near to home, there is something
reminiscent of the "ghastly premises," as Nietzsche
characterizes them, lurking in the plot of classical
tragedy.

The habit of indirection, of circuitous, disguised, or
evasive action, also manifests itself in a pronounced
preference for various forms of "infantile" sexuality.
James's success in dealing with such themes as homosexuality, child-contamination, and so on seems to depend
upon his degree of conscious awareness, hence control of
his theme and its implications. In *The Bostonians*, for
example, James is fully in charge—at least of these
aspects—and we are given a deliberate and compelling
study of Olive Chancellor's lesbianism and its ramifications in the larger society of female Boston reformers. But
in *The Portrait of a Lady*, where the issues of freedom,
choice, and responsibility predominate, there is a strange
lapse, a failure of connection between certain aspects of
Isabel's private experience and these larger issues. Her
narcissism, her frigidity, and the profound sexual terror
she exhibits when Goodwood succeeds in arousing her
remain undealt with, unrelated to the philosophical and
moral motifs of the novel, yet the relation is in fact
integral if not crucial. But because it is avoided by James,
the ending of the book, Isabel's "inexplicable" decision to
return to Osmond, is unsatisfactory and disturbing. The
ostensible explanations offered: that she has made Pansy a
promise; that she has made her own bed (so to speak)
and will lie in it; that it is part of the meaning and nature

of human responsibility to face the consequences of one's own choices, simply fail to be convincing in view of what seems a return to spiritual destitution. It is true that we do not *know* that Isabel might not find within herself enough strength to deal with Osmond, but, if so, we have to take her ability on faith. Furthermore, even if she were able to, it is hard to see, given his character, how the game could be worth the candle. But whether or not James intended to persuade us that it would be, the book still leaves unresolved the connections it raises between sex and morality. It is made very clear in the novel that she is afraid of Goodwood's sexuality, and her decision to return to Osmond is not definite until after the scene when Caspar kisses her in the garden. Whatever James's conscious intentions, the effect is to suggest a connection between these two things. James's evasion of the implications here is one of the few lapses in an otherwise superb novel. The result makes Isabel's collapse seem total and pointless; it becomes an immersion in futility, an apparent loss of will, of courage, of integrity. It is *this* that disagrees, as Strether would put it, with our spiritual stomach; not the suffering, but the banality on which it is based, the absurdity of its cause.

Such collapses of a character's will occur in James occasionally irrespective of any relationship they may have to sexual motifs per se. At times he was simply compelled by the pathos of the suffering, passive figure who (yearningly) renounces life, lets himself be wounded, crushed, or almost absorbed by someone else's will. He took a stand against this tendency in himself (when he complained, for example, that his hero Roderick Hudson had too much of the "principle of collapse") on the grounds that it involved a diminution of dramatic intensity and interest; to achieve these, he felt, there must be some provision for resistance and opposition of the central character to his fate: he (or she) might still be doomed, but not without a struggle.

However one characterizes what I have called James's negative imagination—as a tendency toward renunciation, evasion, indirection, or passive capitulation—it must be examined in terms of its literary effects. There has been an unfortunate tendency all along on the part of James's critics to drag his soul before the rostrum and sit in judgment of it, as if *that* were the issue: There is "no indication that he was capable of love"; [20] he has "let his moral taste slip into abeyance"; "The relation between deficiency of this order [a deficiency in vitality] and the kind of moral unsatisfactoriness that we have observed in *The Golden Bowl* should be fairly plain." [21] What, one wonders, would these critics have to say about the "moral sense" of the author of *Madame Bovary* or of *Troilus and Cressida* or, in relation to "vitality," of *Tamburlaine?*

As we pointed out in the first chapter, it is perfectly true that qualities like "energy directly exhibited" (as James described Tolstoy's work) are not characteristic of James's art. He was primarily interested in certain effects to be achieved by depicting the refraction of reality through the media of several consciousnesses, by radical experiments in architectonics, and by creating a luminous, sensuously metaphorical texture in his works. The "passivity" of certain of his characters is only one of many

[20] W. Somerset Maugham, *The Vagrant Mood: Six Essays* (London, 1952), p. 203.
[21] Leavis, *The Great Tradition*, pp. 196, 205.

factors leading to a certain lustrously disembodied quality that his work sometimes has: much of his art has the effect of dividing our responses and preventing our "full" engagement with the fate—as such—of the characters. The interest is abstract, detached, intellectual rather than directly involved and felt. In some instances, in "The Beast in the Jungle" or in much of *The Golden Bowl,* for example we may find ourselves more responsive to the patterning of events, the formal interplay of ironic reversal, or (in the novel) the richness of texture, than to the actual persons whom the events concern.

Passivity as such is much commoner in his male characters than in his female ones: what activity and vitality there are to be found in his fiction are in fact limited almost exclusively to the women characters. The number of "aggressive" males he depicts can be counted on the fingers of one hand, and they (Caspar Goodwood, Gloriani) are minor actors, functioning mainly as foils for a Gilbert Osmond or Lambert Strether. But the number of aggressive females is considerable: there is scarcely a novel in which the extreme weight of possibility and responsibility is not placed on the women, for good or ill. They are simply all over the place: doves and panther-esses, cool icebergs in some northern sea, Brittanias of the Marketplace and ladies. James's fictional world is domi-nated by females. "She wanted, Susan Shepherd," Merton reflects, "then, as appeared, the same thing Kate wanted. . . . Then Mrs. Lowder wanted, by so odd an evolution of her exuberance, exactly what each of the others did; and he was between them all, he was in the midst. . . . He was glad there was no male witness; it was a circle of petticoats; he should n't have liked a man to see him"

(XX, 209). Then, after Milly's death, in the presence of Sir Luke, he reflects again, "It was just by being a man of the world and by knowing life, by feeling the real, that Sir Luke did him good. There had been, in all the case, too many women. A man's sense of it, another man's, changed the air" (XX, 305). In *The Golden Bowl*, the whole struggle is between Maggie and Charlotte: for possession, for dominance, for victory. The men await the will of their mates and the outcome of the battle for the prize male; for that is what it is, a story of two women fighting for the same man. The man prefers one, but it is the women who make the decision.[22] The society in all three of the last novels, as well as in a number of the earlier ones, is a matriarchy.[23]

The Ambassadors is especially interesting in this respect, for it is the only novel that explicitly articulates the masculine-feminine opposition into contrasting social structures. Even in *The Bostonians*, which deals with the relation between private and public life and has for its theme a battle to the death between the sexes, the only *society* as such is female. But in *The Ambassadors* we have a deliberate delineation of both a matriarchy and a patriarchy: the former the America of the invisible Mrs. Newsome and her husband, the latter the Europe of the

[22] Adam Verver plays an active role, but it is on behalf of his daughter that he does so, and at the considerable cost, to him, of permanent separation from her. It is true that he goes away with his wife at the end, but it is also true that he infinitely prefers his daughter to her.

[23] This word is intended in all but its most technical sense as a system of kinship. In *effect*, however, in the Woollett, Massachusetts, of Mrs. Newsome, the mother is the head of the family, descent is reckoned in the female line, and the children belong to the mother's "clan."

invisible Compte de Vionnet and his wife. When the second group of ambassadors, Sally, Jim, and Mamie Pocock, come from America to accomplish the mission Strether has failed in, he begins to grasp that Jim's function is only decorative:

Jim in fact, he presently made up his mind, was individually out of it; Jim did n't care; Jim had n't come out either for Chad or for him; Jim in short left the moral side to Sally and indeed simply availed himself now, for the sense of recreation, of the fact that he left almost everything to Sally. He was nothing compared to Sally, and not so much by reason of Sally's temper and will as by that of her more developed type and greater acquaintance with the world. He . . . confessed, as he sat there with Strether, that he felt his type hang far in the rear of his wife's and still further, if possible, in the rear of his sister's. Their types, he well knew, were recognised and acclaimed; whereas the most a leading Woollett business-man could hope to achieve socially, and for that matter industrially,[24] was a certain freedom to play into this general glamour.

. . . Pocock was normally and consentingly though not quite wittingly out of the question. It was despite his being normal; it was despite his being cheerful; it was despite his being a leading Woollett business-man. . . . He seemed to say that there was a whole side of life on which the perfectly usual *was* for leading Woollett business-men to be out of the question. . . . Strether's imagination, as always, worked, and he asked himself if this side of life were not somehow connected, for those who figured on it, with the fact of marriage. Would *his* relation to it, had he married ten years before, have become now the same as Pocock's? Might it even become the same should he marry in a few months? Should he ever

[24] Mrs. Newsome controls the business.

know himself as much out of the question for Mrs. Newsome as Jim knew himself—in a dim way—for Mrs. Jim?

   . . . What . . . came home to him . . . at this hour, was that the society over there, that of which Sarah and Mamie—and, in a more eminent way, Mrs. Newsome herself—were specimens, was essentially a society of women, and that poor Jim was n't in it. (XXII, 81–83)

Strether summarizes the role of the male in this woman-bound society as one that exemplifies, simply, "failure of type," which really means failure of individuality, not of generality or typicality. "Small and fat and constantly facetious, straw-coloured and destitute of marks, [Jim] would have been practically indistinguishable had n't his constant preference for light-grey clothes, for white hats, for very big cigars and very little stories, done what it could for his identity" (XXII, 83).

The problem of self, the search for personal significance, is at the very center of Strether's story: the novel has to be seen in part as a comic quest for identity, and primarily sexual identity, even though the quest is obscured under a number of layers of mist and is articulated only indirectly in the book. In a way, *The Ambassadors* is a refined parody of the motifs that Lionel Trilling discusses in his introduction to *The Princess Casamassima:* the Young Man from the Provinces and its cognate, the Sensitive Young Man. Like the first of these, except that he is not young, Strether,

equipped with . . . pride and intelligence . . . stands outside life and seeks to enter. This modern hero is connected with the tales of the folk. Usually his motive is the legendary one of setting out to seek his fortune, which is what the folktale says when it means that the hero is seeking himself. . . .

It is the fate of the Young Man to move from an obscure position to one of considerable eminence, in Paris or London or St. Petersburg, to touch the life of the rulers of the earth. . . . He is confronted by situations whose meanings are dark to him.

And as with the second of these young men, it is Strether's "part merely to be puzzled and hurt"[25] by what he encounters. These legends, and *The Ambassadors*, also contain a pastoral element, a contrast between innocence and corruption, a critique of "court" life. They are stories, too, of sexual initiation, the *rite de passage* into manhood.

The limits and the possibilities of Strether's quest are symbolized, as we have suggested, by the alternatives offered by the two contrasting civilizations and their respective styles of life and attitudes toward life, even their social and political structure. The book works toward two elaborate definitions of the significance that each culture has for Strether. What does he seek, what is his quest *for?* The whole book is a definition or articulation of this, through an intricate process of observation, perception, experience, and association on the part of the searcher, who is a man of divided inclinations.

To be a male in the America of Mrs. Newsome's Woollett, Massachusetts—at least a married male—is to be the second sex; to lack respect, responsibility, authority, and power; to be used for breeding and escort purposes but little else, in short, to lack personal identity. To be a male is to be "out of it," is to be not a type but rather, and precisely, a "failure of type."

[25] (New York, 1948), pp. x–xi.

Whereas the central phenomenon of Strether's European adventure is the very concept itself of "types," the hierarchical ordering of experience. Everything important that happens to him, everything that has any significance at all for him in Europe, is a function of some concrete embodiment of this concept or of something closely associated with it. As we have seen, it is intimate to the notion of taste, or an attitude toward *things* that is selective and qualitative, and to the experience itself of sensuous delight in those things that the imagination selects as worthy of delight. And who is best equipped to exercise the faculty of taste? Who but that type who most compels Strether's fancy, the man of the world. And what is the object best suited to delight his taste? What but that other great work of European art, the *femme du monde*. She, the woman who can look graceful with her elbows on the table, is the central image of desire in the novel, just as Mrs. Newsome (all "cold thought," all "moral pressure") is the central image of the repudiation of desire. Madame de Vionnet moves in a medium of privacy, peace, dignity, and style: the "ancient Paris" that Strether was always looking for and finds objectified by her surroundings. It

was in the immemorial polish of the wide waxed staircase and in the fine *boiseries,* the medallions, mouldings, mirrors, great clear spaces, of the greyish-white salon into which he had been shown. He seemed at the very outset to see her in the midst of possessions not vulgarly numerous, but hereditary cherished charming. . . . He had never before, to his knowledge, had present to him relics, of any special dignity, of a private order. . . . His attention took them all tenderly into account. . . . Chad and Miss Gostrey had rummaged and purchased and picked up and exchanged, sifting, selecting, comparing; whereas the mistress of the scene before him, beautifully passive under the spell of transmission—transmission from her father's line, he quite made up his mind—had only received, accepted and been quiet. (XXI, 243-245)

Her image is explicitly connected with the phenomena of artistry, aristocracy, patriarchy, and these in turn with her compelling sexuality: "At bottom of it all for him was the sense of her rare unlikeness to the women he had known. . . . Everything in fine made her immeasurably new, and nothing so new as the old house and the old objects" (XXI, 246). Strether's Europe presents him, in other words, with diverse realms of experience whose boundaries merge into one another in phantasmagoric fashion, through the process of association, to form a complex symbolic pattern. There is a dreamlike progression from the central concept of "type" through the related concept of taste to the phenomenon of sensuous relish in the immediate flux of experience, which in turn becomes associated in Strether's mind with a kind of golden sensuality, paganism, and uncorrupted sexuality. The last is of course his ardent puritan delusion, his wishful belief in the "virtuous" nature of the attachment between Chad and Madame de Vionnet: Strether wants to make a Paradise of his Paris. His New England conscience is destined to be overthrown twice, once when the delusion is shattered, again when he is forced to acknowledge that virtue is not necessarily equatable with chastity.

In the interim, however, the delusion serves its temporary function of reconciling irreconcilable worlds, of removing the taint of sin from the promise of masculinity. We have said earlier that all of Strether's needs, wishes, and ambivalent response to both civilizations are focused upon Madame de Vionnet and Chad, and more than anything else it is Chad's casual male dominance that attracts and compels Strether. And here again, in the series of revolving mirrors and shifting images by means of which Strether looks at Chad, we find the same progression from one realm of experience to another. Chad is "a gentleman," which is to say "a man of the world," "a young man marked out by women," "an irreducible young Pagan" (XXI, 156–157). There is no "failure of type" here, but a kind of lush abundance of alternative yet equivalent categories of identity in which being a gentleman is somehow the same as being a pagan. Chad is Strether's noble savage, his prefallen Adam; it is above all Chad's "romantic privilege" that he envies him, the privilege of having been young and happy in the charged air of Paris among the "delicate and appetising" effects of tone and tint, of having "the common, unattainable art of taking things as they come," of demonstrating in his person "some sense of power . . . something latent and beyond access, ominous and perhaps enviable" (XXI, 156).

And the society that has made this possible is a society in which prerogatives and authority are vested in the male. Madame de Vionnet's marriage was arranged for her; she had no option, no recourse. In turn, Chad arranges the marriage of her daughter—at the very time when Woollett wishes him home not only for reasons of business but, more important, to "marry him off," and when Mrs. Newsome has taken the first steps in selecting his mate for him by sending Mamie Pocock along.[26] Indeed, the striking contrast between the young girls produced by each culture is illuminating in this respect: Jeanne de Vionnet, *jeune fille*, delicate, charming, passive, perfectly obedient, and Mamie Pocock, already portly, mature, standing perpetually in the receiving line.

The great symbol of the male prerogative in this European civilization is the Catholic Church, that most organized of patriarchies. We have already seen that for Waymarsh the Church is emblematic of the intrinsic treachery of Europe: the "enemy," the "monster," the "multiplication of shibboleths . . . rank with feudalism," whose hierarchical ordering of the universe represents the grossest dangers to the free democratic spirit. The Church means "society" to Waymarsh and the "discrimination of types." We have seen the intricate associations that led from "mere discriminations about a pair of gloves" on Strether's part to fear of the "loss of his immortal soul": associations proceeding, once again, from the concept of "type" to that of taste, to enjoyment of sensuous particularity, from there to the hidden serpent lust buried in Europe's bosom; the American equation of sophistication with wickedness.

It is significant therefore to look at Strether's associations when he meets the great artist Gloriani in the company of ladies and gentlemen "in whose liberty to be as they were [Strether] was aware that he positively rejoiced." The scene, in a spacious garden attached to old noble houses with delicate and rare decorations, speaks to

[26] Further, it is Mamie who decides she doesn't want Chad, not the other way around.

Strether "of survival, transmission, association, a strong
indifferent persistent order" (XXI, 195). The open air in
these conditions seems "a chamber of state," and he
presently has "the sense of a great convent, a convent of
missions, famous for he scarce knew what, a nursery of
young priests, of scattered shade, of straight alleys and
chapel-bells, that spread its mass in one quarter; he had
the sense of names in the air, of ghosts at the windows, of
signs and tokens, a whole range of expression, all about
him, too thick for prompt discrimination" (XXI, 196).

Gloriani, Chad, Waymarsh, and little Bilham each in
his way represents success to Strether, and each functions
in the role of alter ego for him, but none so intensely as the
great sculptor, "with his genius in his eyes, his manners on
his lips, his long career behind him and his honours all
round." During their brief encounter, with the sculptor's
eyes holding his, Strether experiences a revelation about
Gloriani that is at the same time a profound self-exposure;
he is at a loss to know whether he has been told something
or asked something. In fact, both things have occurred:
each man has taken the measure of the other. The
difficulty for poor Strether is his consciousness of how
little there is in himself to be measured, either successful
personal relationships or achievement in the affairs of
men. But Gloriani represents both. Where Strether had
dreamed in his youth of forming a relation with the
higher culture and raising up the "temple of taste,"
Gloriani's accomplishments are realities, not broken
dreams; with that "most special flare, unequalled, supreme, of the aesthetic torch, lighting that wondrous
world for ever" (XXI, 197), he is "a dazzling prodigy of
type" (XXI, 196), the great artist. And where "it was

absolutely true" of Strether that "even after the close of
the period of conscious detachment occupying the centre
of his life, the grey middle desert of the two deaths, that
of his wife and that, ten years later, of his boy—he had
never taken any one anywhere" (XXI, 52), Gloriani is
surrounded by *femmes du monde;* there is "deep human
expertness in [his] charming smile—of, the terrible life
behind it!" (XXI, 197); he is "the glossy male tiger,
magnificently marked" (XXI, 219).

This vision of Gloriani is the apotheosis of Strether's
European adventure. The artist is the exalted image of the
complex set of personal possibilities—ones, however, that
only *might* have been, represented by Europe for
Strether, who is reduced to murmuring helplessly after
their encounter, "Oh, if everything had been different!"
The whole novel, as has been mentioned, is an elaborate
definition of what constitutes that "everything," but all
the intricate associations making up the definition are
condensed and fused in the figure of Gloriani: Strether's
longing for release from both avoidance and caution
(which is his definition of personal freedom) so that he
might enjoy the thing of the moment, take things as they
come, satiate his appetite for beautiful things, even smoke
with a woman. The latter of course is a thinly disguised
version of the male tiger's activities: one must always with
Strether's remarks about himself read behind the obscur-
ing veil dropped by his New England conscience. But no
matter what the devious routes, mazes and metaphors,
elaborate veneers of civilization, all the paths in this novel
lead finally to the jungle (Strether's word).[27] With

[27] "Were they, this pair [Madame de Vionnet and Gloriani], of
the 'great world'?—and was he himself, for the moment and thus re-

whatever overlays of ambivalence, the ordeal of sexuality is *the* major theme of *The Ambassadors.*

This ambivalence is of course conscious, intentional: we are warned at the outset of the oddity of Strether's double nature; he is intended to be the embodiment of the reluctant puritan, hating his own "odious ascetic suspicion of any form of beauty," labeling with the word "failure" the general inability to enjoy that is one of Woollett's main characteristics, recognizing with an inward chill that Mrs. Newsome is "all cold thought" or "all moral pressure." The drama of the novel is meant to be a drama of self-division. Strether dips his toe, so to speak, in the unholy waters of Babylon but remains shivering, and peeping, on the bank while others take the plunge for him. This insistent yet somewhat shady, or voyeuristic, timorousness is typical of James's sensitive male protagonists and here is superbly faithful to the novel's study of the New England conscience and the American puritan temperament, one characteristic of which is precisely the combination of rectitude of behavior and lasciviousness of thought. It is a diabolic twosome, as Hawthorne knows, and shows so well in "The Minister's Black Veil," where the man of God imagines sin where none exists and himself becomes the profound emblem of righteous dirty-mindedness. Similarly, when in their initial interview, Chad denies that he is or ever was "entangled," Strether asks,

---

lated to them by his observation, *in* it? Then there was something in the great world covertly tigerish, which came to him across the lawn and in the charming air as a waft from the jungle" (XXI, 219).

"Then what are you here for? What has kept you? . . . if you *have* been able to leave?"

It made Chad, after a stare, throw himself back. "Do you think one's kept only by women?" His surprise and his verbal emphasis rang out so clear in the still street that Strether winced till he remembered the safety of their English speech. "Is that," the young man demanded, "what they think at Woollett?" At the good faith in the question Strether had changed colour, feeling that, as he would have said, he had put his foot in it. He had appeared stupidly to misrepresent what they thought at Woollett; but before he had time to rectify Chad again was upon him. "I must say then you show a low mind." (XXI, 159)

It is of course what they think at Woollett, and there has been no misrepresentation except as Strether would feel, in the spirit of the thing: Woollett is after all indignant, not acquiescent, and the filth isn't their own imagining (he imagines): Chad *is* being kept by a woman. As indeed he is; Strether's ethical re-education in Europe eventually leads him to the point where he ceases to make the automatic equation between sex and sin, at least for others. But for himself the two sides of the dialectic remain unsynthesized, and the real end result of his adventures is to render America and Europe both unfit abodes for his soul. Furthermore, such an outcome is absolutely characteristic of James. It is intrinsic to his imaginative vision of things to see the world as rent asunder, with half its goods on the left hand of God, half on the right, and no passage in between. But what is more uniquely Jamesian, since most serious literature deals in dichotomy, opposition, and paradox, is that the negative sides of his dilemmas are the ones that speak the loudest and hold final sway. This is true of him beyond logic, and so consistently true that it amounts to a compulsive orientation to existence; at the very least a repetitive stance of negation. For there is nothing inherent in the logical structure of a dilemma that makes defeat a necessity. There is only one necessity in a genuine dilemma, and that is compromise, or the sacrifice of what one hopes is the lesser good for the sake of keeping the greater. And it is just this necessity that the Jamesian character typically rejects. Strether, Kate Croy, Milly Theale, and even Merton Densher, each in his way, all want the best of both possible worlds, the best, or nothing. There is a latent but insistent streak of romanticism in James that manifests itself in this characteristic rejection of the limitations that are inherent in every human situation. It has long been recognized by critics, and usually with considerable irritation, that James releases his characters from the ordinary burdens of economic necessity (Adam Verver is a multimillionaire, Isabel Archer is left a massive fortune in the first flush of her youth, Milly Theale is "the heiress of all the ages," and even Strether has "enough" that it is a matter concern to him to select an heir), but it has been less well recognized that he endows these same characters with the impulse to be free from all necessity and restriction. When Madame Merle tells Isabel that the clothes one wears, the books one reads, the company one keeps are all the palpable expressions of one's self, Isabel demurs:

"I don't agree with you. I think just the other way. I don't know whether I succeed in expressing myself, but I know that nothing else expresses me. Nothing that belongs to me is any measure of me; everything's on the contrary a limit, a barrier, and a perfectly arbitrary one. Certainly the clothes which, as you say, I choose to wear, don't express me; and heaven forbid they should!"

"You dress very well," Madame Merle lightly interposed.

"Possibly; but I don't care to be judged by that. My clothes may express the dressmaker, but they don't express me. To begin with it's not my own choice that I wear them; they're imposed upon me by society."

"Should you prefer to go without them?" Madame Merle enquired in a tone which virtually terminated the discussion.[28]

But Isabel is not the only rebel against barriers; Kate, Milly, Charlotte, Maggie, even poor hesitant Strether all have immortal longings, all resist to the last degree of their energy the acknowledgment that the world either is not, or cannot be made into, the image of their own desires. The pattern that follows the acknowledgment is that of renunciation if not collapse: Isabel returning to Osmond; Strether a permanent exile from both landscapes of his soul; Charlotte whimpering like a wounded animal, being led to America by an "invisible noose," a silken cord in her husband's hand; the Prince docile and impotent awaiting his wife's pleasure; Milly turning her face to the wall.

James's own definition of romance centers precisely upon this phenomenon of the limits, the conditions that attend experience.

The only *general* attribute of projected romance that I can see, the only one that fits all its cases, is the fact of the kind of

[28] Henry James, *The Portrait of a Lady*, New York ed.; vols. II–III (New York, 1908), III, 288.

experience with which it deals—experience liberated, so to speak; experience disengaged, disembroiled, disencumbered, exempt from the conditions that we usually know to attach to it and, if we wish so to put the matter, drag upon it, and operating in a medium which relieves it . . . of the inconvenience of a *related,* a measurable state, a state subject to all our vulgar communities. . . . The balloon of experience is in fact of course tied to the earth, and under that necessity we swing, thanks to a rope of considerable length, in the more or less commodious car of the imagination; but it is by the rope we know where we are, and from the moment that cable is cut we are at large and unrelated; we only swing apart from the globe—though remaining as exhilarated, naturally, as we like, especially when all goes well. The art of the romancer is, "for the fun of it," insidiously to cut the cable, to cut it without our detecting him.[29]

Isabel would understand her creator's metaphor: her own imagery of life is not unlike it.

"Do you know where you are going, Isabel Archer?"

"Just now I'm going to bed," said Isabel with persistent frivolity.

"Do you know where you're drifting?" Henrietta pursued. . . .

"No, I have n't the least idea, and I find it very pleasant not to know. A swift carriage, of a dark night, rattling with four horses over roads that one can't see—that's my idea of happiness." [30]

Even the unusual severity of the conditions that in fact attend the lives and possibilities of these characters (what after all does one do when one discovers that one's

[29] *The Art of the Novel,* pp. 33–34.
[30] *The Portrait of a Lady,* III, 235.

husband and stepmother are lovers? or that a mortal illness can only be interrupted by falling in love?) is itself a romantic phenomenon, paradoxical though it may seem. For the very severity is an idealization: not so much improbable [31] as extraordinary and uncontrolled, as James would say, "by our general sense of 'the way things happen.'" The tests are severer, the pain intenser and at the same time more "exalted" than we would ordinarily expect to find even in the difficult aspects of our everyday lives. So that what we discover again and again in the dramatic situation of these novels is a group of characters whose unusually strong impulse to reject restriction must act itself out in a situation that is unusually restricted. The process of avoiding a choice between one set of possibilities and another, in other words of compromising, may vary from person to person—Strether and Milly deceive themselves about the nature of the reality around them, Densher deludes himself about the nature of his own actions, Kate simply denies that a dilemma exists—but the essential phenomenon is the same in each case and consists of a refusal to make peace with reality, to accept or even to acknowledge the limitations that are a part of every human situation. And this is a characteristic of "hero" and "villain" alike in James's world: both types are overreachers. The difference between them is in the nature of their illusions, not in their fundamental denial of reality. Thus the characteristic illusion of the Jamesian villain is that he may with impunity get what he wants simply by taking it regardless of who else may suffer in the process, and the characteristic illusion of the hero is that no one would ever harm

[31] That is, we do not disbelieve in the situations.

him for the sake of gain, or for any other reason. Both types have an extraordinary faith in appearances: the latter typically believes that appearances are all there is, that the world *is* the way it seems, the former that appearances are all that matters, that immunity from retribution is automatically achieved by protective coloration. Thus the great deceivers in the novels—Madame Merle and Osmund, Kate and Densher and Aunt Maud, Chad and Madame de Vionnet, Charlotte and the Prince —all take pains to keep their social masks flawless: polished, perfect and automatic. The golden bowl has a crack, a flaw, but great care is taken by the author to make it clear to us that the flaw is *imperceptible,* invisible to the naked, certainly to the untrained, inexpert eye.

The basic pattern of all these novels is the same; it consists of the gradual undeception of protagonist and antagonist alike, but always after irrevocable harm has been done. The same painful lessons are learned too late again and again by both camps on the battlefield. Kate's final word to her lover, and the note on which the book closes, is "we shall never be again as we were!" (XX, 405); and Madame de Vionnet's final interview with Strether wrings from her the admission that she has made a change in his life:

"I've upset everything in your mind as well; in your sense of—what shall I call it?—all the decencies and possibilities. It gives me a kind of detestation . . . of everything, of life. . . . What I hate is myself—when I think that one has to take so much, to be happy, out of the lives of others, and that one is n't happy even then. One does it to cheat one's self and to stop one's mouth—but that's only at the best for a little. The wretched self is always there, always making one somehow a fresh anxiety. What it comes to is that it's not, that it's never, a happiness, any happiness at all, to *take*. The only safe thing is to give. It's what plays you least false." (XXII, 282–283)

But if there is never any happiness in taking, neither is there in the determined pretense that takers are absent from the world. James's victims share the burden of responsibility with their victimizers, and the events of the novels must be seen as a kind of cooperative venture in pain. The "guilt" of Isabel, Milly, Strether, and Maggie is a wilful blindness, a staggering self-deception based upon wishful thinking. The victims in each case wish to believe in the appearance put forth by those who practice upon them; their cases are complementary, and the responsibility is divided. James's finest talent in a way is for seeing what will not work. He is the most unsentimental of our great romanticists.

CHAPTER IV

The Golden Bowl

THE GOLDEN BOWL [1] is at once the most intense and least *related*—James's own term for experience "subject to all our vulgar communities"—of the last three novels. The major characters are a beautiful woman, a prince, a princess, and a billionaire. These indeed are the only characters, aside from one other couple of importance and a handful of occasional guests. The humor that makes *The Ambassadors* a major novel of social satire, and that is still considerable in *The Wings of the Dove*, is rare in *The Golden Bowl*. What humor there is focuses upon the muted vaudeville performances of Colonel Assingham and his wife in front of no audience but

---

[1] New York ed., vols. XXIII–XXIV (New York, 1909). Citations from *The Golden Bowl* in my text are to this edition.

themselves: "He had again and again sat up late to discuss those situations in which her finer consciousness abounded, but he had never failed to deny that anything in life, anything of hers, could be a situation for himself" (XXIII, 64–65). The source of the humor is the vagaries and exaggerations of their private relationship, with Colonel Bob playing the straight man to his wife's flights of insight, imagination of disaster, and compulsive meddlings in the lives of her friends:

He edited for their general economy the play of her mind, just as he edited, savingly, with the stump of a pencil, her redundant telegrams. . . .

Mrs. Assingham denied, as we know, that her husband had a play of mind; so that she could, on her side, treat [his] remarks only as if they had been senseless physical gestures or nervous facial movements. She overlooked them as from habit and kindness; yet there was no one to whom she talked so persistently of such intimate things. (XXIII, 67–68)

So we are provided with a built-in "comic" situation, the form of which is persistence in the face of apparent misunderstanding. The setting is private, the tone intimate, the audience no one but the actors themselves, and the content an elaborate effort on Fanny's part to divest herself of the responsibility attendant on being a tamperer. Only the latter has implications beyond the nature of their personal relationship and in the broader social context of the novel. That context itself is narrower and deeper and more solitary than in the preceding works; reminiscent, in its sense of isolation and fanatical inwardness, of "The Beast in the Jungle," "The Turn of the Screw," and *The Sacred Fount;* whereas *The Ambassadors,* in spite of obvious differences, still shares an important kinship with *The Bostonians*. It is no accident therefore that there is little free play of wit across a broad spectrum of social forms, attitudes, manners in *The Golden Bowl*, no Woollett, Massachusetts, "represented by a Mamie . . . bland . . . bridal . . . and almost disconcertingly reassuring." The portraits in this novel are ones in depth, not breadth, in spite of the use once again of the international theme, the clash of representatives from the New and Old Worlds. For these representatives themselves are more like mythological heroes of legendary cultures than "ambassadors" of specific places. James's imagination tends toward a higher and higher degree of abstraction in each of the three novels. Most of the characters in *The Ambassadors* fall into familiar slots of sophisticated society: the man of the world, the *jeune fille*, the *femme du monde*, the great artist, the Bohemian, the American businessman on a toot in Paris, the young American Girl. In *The Wings of the Dove*, however, the latter becomes the "heiress of all the ages," a "princess," and a "New York legend of affecting, of romantic isolation," while still recognizable, in her innocence, directness, and instinct for pleasing in unexpected ways, as the American Girl. Merton, while "not unamenable, on certain sides, to classification—as for instance by being a gentleman," still fails "to play straight into an observer's hands. He was young for the House of Commons, he was loose for the army. He was refined, as might have been said, for the City and, quite apart from the cut of his cloth, he was sceptical, it might have been felt, for the Church." And because he is "too much" this or that to be pigeonholed, he represents "above all . . . that wondrous state of youth" (XIX, 49) still unformed, still in the process of fermentation, still without its final stamp. And just as Milly is a "New York legend," Aunt Maud is a London one. She is "Britannia of the Market Place," but she belongs in a still more general category too, because she is dangerous: "Yet what were the dangers, after all, but just the dangers of life and of London? Mrs. Lowder *was* London, *was* life—the roar of the siege and the thick of the fray. There were some things, after all, of which Britannia was afraid; but Aunt Maud was afraid of nothing" (XIX, 31–32).

Furthermore, the "New York" of which Milly is a legend is itself a legendary kind of place: it is not even second cousin to Woollett, Massachusetts, in which we have the deliberate portrait of a matriarchal, puritan, isolationist village in New England and the appropriate rites and rituals thereof. But Milly's New York is not the urban counterpart of the little Massachusetts manufacturing town. In this "city" there are no defined modes of behavior, manners, occupations, or even people, but simply suggestive evocations, auras, qualities, not to be separated from those of the heroine herself: bereavement on a scale so vast—the effect is that of a total depopulation or evacuation—that only the world's largest city "confused . . . but multitudinous" could contain it; financial possibilities ("masses of money") equally vast; much strangeness and no consolation. It takes Boston, in this geographical scheme of the soul, to provide the latter, for Boston is the one place to help you "really to feel your situation as grave" (XIX, 105) under the discipline of life or of death.

Yet in spite of the dreamlike, almost ghostly image of the metropolis, its use as a symbol of both isolation and acquisition is firmly grounded in American cultural realities of the most familiar and grimmest sort. The legend is usually tied to fact in James, at least at some points along the earth, but his concern is increasingly with interior landscapes and geographies. The "facts" have relevance to him only as they bear upon the latter. These facts—the details of custom, the aspects of behavior and attitude that are culturally determined— become fewer as we progress from *The Ambassadors* through *The Golden Bowl,* but they also become intenser. And what few there are operate as permanent touchstones that measure and dominate the quality of everything within the horizon of the imaginative world presented. It may be one purpose of a given novel to show how deeply unreliable the standard of measure is as a criterion for human happiness, but this does not obliterate the pervasive, almost corrosive, presence of the touchstone itself. The wealth of Adam Verver, and to a lesser degree that of Milly Theale, are cases in point: the massive fortunes of each provide at one and the same time the link to reality and the link to unreality in the respective novels; the place where the balloon of experience is tied to earth, and the shears that cut its rope.

James's ignorance of the business world, at least before his visit to America in 1904–1905, has provoked those among his critics—by far the majority—who have insisted upon bringing the standards of the realistic novel to bear upon a mode of art whose aims were increasingly at variance with those involved in rendering the texture of ordinary daily life. In such works as *The Sacred Fount,* and above all *The Golden Bowl,* James's concern is almost exclusively with the objectification of forms of consciousness. The "real" world obtrudes itself upon the latter novel by means of elaborate metaphors and symbols which are precisely the mode of that objectification. Things, objects in their sensuous particularity—the architecture of both the natural and social world—are vividly represented, but as analogues for the shifting states of mind, patterns of perception of the character (or other narrator) through whose eyes the story is seen:

This situation [Maggie's relation to her father and her connection with her husband, who, though she does not know it yet, is having an affair with her stepmother] had been occupying for months and months the very centre of the garden of her life, but it had reared itself there like some strange tall tower of ivory, or perhaps rather some wonderful beautiful but outlandish pagoda, a structure plated with hard bright porcelain, coloured and figured and adorned at the overhanging eaves with silver bells that tinkled ever so charmingly when stirred by chance airs. (XXIV, 3)

In *The Ambassadors*, the perceiving consciousness is more "transparent'" in the sense that it finds its symbolic correspondences in scenes, situations, or objects from an external world posited as "real" (for example, Strether's Paris) within the confines of the novel, rather than finding them exclusively in vivid metaphors of its own imagining. But even in *The Ambassadors*, James is not concerned with rendering what is "out there" for it own sake [2] (one of the avowed if mythical aims of "realistic" fiction). He is concerned rather with depicting the ways in which what is out there "demonstrates" the mind that is perceiving it. Therefore, to apply standards (in this case ones like

[2] Though James delights in the sensuous texture of the external world.

verisimilitude in the depiction of details from everyday life) that are totally irrelevant to the nature and aims of James's late art is not only to misjudge that art but literally to mis-see it. The critical reaction to *The Golden Bowl*—preponderantly negative—comes from a reluctance, almost phobic in nature, not only to grant the artist his premises but even to see what they are to begin with. *The Golden Bowl* is radical, extreme, modern. It persistently has been judged by standards irrelevant not only to itself but to modern art in general and, in significant ways, all art.

The critics have come down heavily in the case of Adam Verver in particular:

James was always ready to confess that he did not have the shadowiest notion of business; but by picking a character like Adam Verver he obligated himself to some knowledge of the type of men who were making the great American fortunes. . . . Mr. Verver's moral tone is far more like that of a benevolent Swedenborgian than it is like that of either John D. Rockefeller or Jay Gould.[3]

Assuming that James's work addresses itself to the faithful depiction of the economic and cultural realities of his time, they have condemned the delineation of Verver out of hand, finding it impossible to reconcile his history of acquisition with his blandness (a much more cryptic quality in Adam than they acknowledge) and sweetness of character.

But James is not interested in giving us a realistic picture of a John D. Rockefeller, the conditions that he created, or the conditions that created him. The figure of

[3] F. O. Matthiessen, *Henry James: The Major Phase* (New York, 1944), pp. 89–90.

the millionaire caught James's imagination—as did the notion of "the American"—because of certain suggestive qualities it symbolized. One of these is the capacity for ruthlessness (Adam is not merely benevolent), a form of intensity and single-mindedness of purpose that James calls "monotony." Another is the power of immense wealth to exempt people from the "conditions we usually know to attach" to experience. And though Adam combines the predatory or acquisitive instincts of the man who has made his own fortune with the highly developed taste and selectivity of any "collector," James conceived of him as larger than life, an alchemist not to be evaluated by ordinary criteria. He was a case of "a special genius"; the "chamber of his brain" was a "strange workshop of fortune . . . mysterious and almost anonymous" (XXIII, 127).

But, on another level, the book has, as Philip Rahv remarks, "the enormous vitality which springs from the actual dreamlife of a social class—a dream of the 'loot of empire,' an imperial dream full of 'real' objects and 'real' life. One can object to its content on ideological grounds, and on those grounds James is indeed vulnerable [here, notice, Rahv too slips back into evaluating the novel from the perspective of social criticism, which is too bad because he otherwise beautifully captures an essential quality of the novel]; but one cannot deny that it is historically meaningful and that it has interest and artistry and a kind of meditated though cruel beauty."[4]

The vision in this book *is* cruel, it *is* meditated, and in its own context it is as rapacious as any nightmare of Dreiser's. The fact that Adam is initially presented to us

[4] *Image and Idea* (Norfolk, Connecticut, 1957), p. 82.

dressed in the robes of a saint and that Maggie is compared to the Virgin, only intensifies the horror of what finally happens inside these people as well as to them. To be misled about the inner transformations of Maggie and her father is to miss the very heart of the novel itself, its vision of ravage and woe and brutality. James shares with Dreiser a profound involvement with the *phenomena* of cruelty, corruption, and exploitation, which both of them see as integral to the human situation. The difference is that Dreiser sees them as removable, as a function of social conditions, whereas James believes quite the opposite: the "conditions," and everything else, are a function, a manifestation of the troubled depths of the human spirit, engaged against itself in internecine struggle. "Everything's terrible, cara—in the heart of man."

The source of pain is internal, yet James is no traditional moralist and the question of will, the free exercise of deliberate choice, becomes so modified in his handling of it that it almost ceases to be relevant. So Milly's option—"She could live if she would"—translates itself instantly into the alternative "She would live if she could," and after each possibility appears a kind of cosmic question mark: Is this right? *Is this?* So Madame de Vionnet can utter, "It's not . . . it's never, a happiness, any happiness at all, to *take*. The only safe thing is to give. It's what plays you least false" (XXII, 282–283). But the sanction is merely what brings the smallest amount of grief and, in spite of Strether's temporary severity with her, the pointlessness, even absurdity, of blaming such a creature is quite clear in the book. Even Strether finally can "think of nothing but the passion, mature, abysmal, pitiful, she represented" (XXII, 286).

Yet the sense of diabolic necessity so strongly implicit in the reactions of Milly, Strether,[5] and Maggie, as well as Kate, Charlotte, and the Prince, is illusory too. These people all feel as if they had, or have, no option, but Strether's caverns are projections of the soul and everything that happens to Milly, the author insists, constitutes what she should have known. So that the final solace of those who despair—blaming the malignant universe—is denied them too. The ultimate loneliness of these books consists in just this: that there is no one and nothing to blame and yet no one is blameless. This is why Strether's strongest need after everything has come out is "a sense—which the spirit required, rather ached and sighed in the absence of—that somebody was paying something somewhere and somehow, that they were at least not all floating together on the silver stream of impunity" (XXII, 272). And he has a terrified perception that perhaps after all it is not true that "the state of the wrongdoer, or at least this person's happiness, presented some special difficulty." Merton, similarly, "in default of being right with himself . . . had meanwhile . . . the interest of seeing—and quite for the first time in his life—whether, on a given occasion, that might be quite so necessary to happiness as was commonly assumed and as he had up to this moment never doubted" (XX, 183).

All of this is important in relation to *The Golden Bowl* because that book, in the process of exploring ramifications of consciousness, challenges the ethical basis of

---

[5] Strether has, he says, "moved among miracles. It was all phantasmagoric" (XXII, 301). And the reckoning to come, which may "be one and the same thing with extinction," faces him while he floats to it "duly through these caverns of Kubla Khan" (XXII, 293).

human life more deeply than either of its predecessors and yet at the same time, critics have felt, more obscurely. In fact the book is not obscure, though the intensity and the seeming unrelatedness of the kind of experience being dealt with, plus the modes of apprehending that experience, combine to give an illusion of impenetrability, fantasy, dream to all that happens. The intensity springs primarily from the situation, each element of which plays a fateful role: the fact that the betrayed partners of the adultery are father and daughter; that father and daughter in turn have a passionate attachment to each other; that the daughter and her stepmother, who is her sexual rival in two senses, are the same age and were friends from girlhood. It is a *ménage à quatre,* or *à cinq* if one includes Fanny Assingham, who is puppet master of the whole show, with the additional burden of a familial setting. And that such a situation, ripe by its very nature for the strongest yet most ambiguous loves, involvements, rivalries, occurs in a near social vacuum contributes to the intensity. For although the Ververs sit at the top of the social ladder, on "a platform looking down, if one would, on the kingdoms of the earth and with standing-room for but half a dozen others" (XXIII, 131), other people are irrelevant to them. When occasionally they intrude, or are even invited to intrude, they become props, adjuncts, extensions of the situation in which the four main characters are involved.

Essentially these four are isolated: unconcerned with anyone but themselves and wealthy enough to indulge their desire for privacy and to live as expatriates without retaliation of any kind from the external world. These phenomena are interrelated, and they are further connected to the particular kind of experience, experience at once detached and intense, that the novel is dealing with. If the kind of question Dreiser asks in his fiction is, "What happens to an individual when he is caught up in the vast economic machinery of our industrial society?" the kind of question James asks is, in effect, "What happens when he is not—when he is freed from the contingencies that ordinarily impinge upon our lives and seem to shape and determine our destiny?" This wish to liberate someone is explicit in *The Portrait of a Lady:* it is Ralph's motive in securing a fortune for Isabel.

"I should like," he tells his father, "to put a little wind in her sails."

"What do you mean by that?"

"I should like to put it into her power to do some of the things she wants. . . . I should like to put money in her purse. . . . I should like to make her rich."

"What do you mean by rich?"

"I call people rich when they're able to meet the requirements of their imagination. Isabel has a great deal of imagination. . . . If she has an easy income she'll never have to marry for a support. That's what I want cannily to prevent. She wishes to be free, and your bequest will make her free." [6]

In exactly the same way Milly Theale, Adam and Maggie Verver, along with Isabel the "victims" of their respective novels, are free to meet the requirements of their imagination. As we have indicated, one of the main functions of wealth in these books is as a device to throw those requirements into high relief, unobscured by other

[6] *The Portrait of a Lady,* New York ed., Vol. III (New York, 1908), pp. 260–261.

demands or necessities. At the same time the sense that the Ververs and their *sposi* are swimming in golden waters intensifies the fantastical, dreamlike effect of the events that are taking place. Adam has plundered the Golden Isles,[7] we are told. His almost immeasurable fortune thus represents the wish-fulfillment of all imperialistic civilizations at any period of time on any part of the globe, whether that of Kubla Khan, of sixteenth-century Spain or England, or nineteenth-century America. We are given a racial not just a national dream of conquest, acquisition, and plunder. And this fact in turn should make more meaningful the deliberate use of the fairy-tale motif in both *The Golden Bowl* and *The Wings of the Dove,* with their princes, princesses, godmothers, and wizards selecting among the "Kingdoms of the Earth" (a phrase used in both novels). *The Golden Bowl* indeed follows with considerable exactness, however unconsciously, the prototype of the fairy tale of "three wishes," in which the third wish[8] is reserved for undoing the first two, which always, no matter what yearnings they have satiated, have

[7] It is worth noting that the two explicit literary references in this novel are to Poe's *Narrative of Arthur Gordon Pym* and Keats's sonnet "On First Looking into Chapman's *Homer.*" The former becomes an image for the Prince, the latter for Adam.

[8] The closest rendering of such a tale in American literature is Hawthorne's version of the King Midas myth for children. Midas, although wealthy, is insatiable. The only thing he loves more than gold is his daughter. Finally granted the wish that whatever he touches may turn to gold he is at first delighted as his bed sheets and roses turn to the precious metal. But then so does his breakfast as he tries to eat and, inevitably, his daughter, who becomes a little frozen statue. In despair, he is granted his wish that the Golden Touch be taken away from him. (Nathaniel Hawthorne, *A Wonder Book* [Garden City, New York], pp. 47–67, no date.)

put the wisher in a state of danger or, more commonly, loss, isolation, alienation from his kind. The two wishes granted the Ververs are extraordinary wealth and extraordinary mates. The causal connection between the two is of course James's own twist. But the result, loss of the earlier, insufficiently recognized bliss, is the same. The price Maggie and her father pay for their greed is permanent separation from each other and the tainting of what remains to them.

But this use of the mythological and archetypical, of dream wealth and fairy-tale marriages, does not make the events of the book obscure, however it may make its tone at once fabulous and somnolent, sinister and immune. What actually happens in the novel is clear enough: a wife who discovers she is being betrayed sets out to recapture her husband at any cost other than that of shattering appearances, and does so. The adjuncts to this "story," which in total effect supersede it, comprise the reasons for the betrayal, the nature of Maggie's response to it, the methods she chooses to combat it, the ultimate havoc these methods wreak on all concerned. And all of these things are clear enough too, in the sense that they can be stated, summarized, discussed.

The complexity of this book in other words does not rest in what happens but in the meaning of what happens, in the attitudes and responses to life that lie behind the kinds of action that take place. These responses are not single. They are deeply ambivalent and divided. The same people are viewed at one and the same time with love and with hatred, with sympathy and with aversion, with pity and with dread. This is why the novel continually eludes the grasp of readers desiring, or expecting, an autonomous vision and helps to account for the violently opposed interpretations given of it. Moreover, James carries the process of exploring the profound inner contradictions of the human psyche further than he has ever done before. In both *The Ambassadors* and *The Wings of the Dove* we have seen the intuitive recognition that the victim plays his part, however unwilfully, in the vast interlocking machinery of human guilt: both Strether and Milly are self-deceived, wish to be deceived because of the promise of paradise that seems to lie within their grasp. Neither can bear to compromise that possibility. The truth necessitates compromise, and so both avoid the truth until it breaks in on them willy-nilly. When it does, when their own visions are shattered, there is just the suggestion in each case of a passive version of retaliation: Strether's suffering and renunciation, which have their effects upon Madame de Vionnet; and Milly's unbearable generosity in after all leaving her fortune to Merton, which has its effect upon him. R. P. Blackmur refers to this in his introduction to *The Golden Bowl:*

In each novel, too, the hero or heroine, across the gap of loneliness, works permanent ravage and ruin, the shameless punishment and the shameful penance of passion upon itself, on the couples who have been enduring illicit love however lovely or natural or treacherous to the point of mere lust (Venus without Cupid, as Montaigne says) the lust had been. Chad Newsome and Marie de Vionnet separate forever. . . . Merton Densher and Kate Croy . . . are riven by the woe of their very humanity, and Amerigo, the Prince, and Charlotte Verver create a lie between themselves which will separate them ocean-wide forever.[9]

[9] (New York, 1952), p. viii.

These remarks must be qualified, though they are suggestive of the central moral movements of the novels. For one thing they do not take sufficiently into account the roles the heroines or heroes themselves play in the consummation of their own deception. For another, they overlook differences in the degree and even kind of suffering, "penance" endured by the illicit lovers. Chad, for example, emerges almost unscathed from his affair: he's off, apparently without remorse, to advertising, Woollett, and if not Mamie then some other sweet young thing at home. Marie de Vionnet, however, endures the pangs of both conscience and passion. Merton suffers more from a sense of penance than Kate Croy does, yet he loses less in the final analysis because he has replaced her image quite effectively with that of Milly; nor does he deny it when Kate tells him he is in love with Milly's memory. Charlotte suffers, in the final analysis, the most of anyone in *The Golden Bowl*, certainly more than the Prince. She loves more, she is banished to a land she both dreads and hates, in the company of an iron-willed man who has put a silken "noose" about her neck and yet a man who, there is more than a slight suggestion, is impotent. Furthermore, Charlotte remains deceived to the very end. In each case the women bear the brunt of loss and of suffering.

Finally, Blackmur's remarks remain too formally within the Christian framework of sin and penance to account for certain elements in the response of the victims, especially Maggie, to those who have betrayed them. He sees *The Golden Bowl* in terms of those who are guilty and those who are innocent, and God's scourge appearing in the form of innocence outraged. Maggie sees herself this way too, but the total effect of her actions does not sustain such a vision. She moves too much in paths of darkness to be credible as a creature of glory and beatitude. In one sense, she behaves as any woman would who is trying to hang on to her husband: she is ruthless. She is a Milly Theale who does not turn her face to the wall, or a Milly risen from the dead to confound her betrayers. And she achieves her practical victory. Yet she is presented as continually having to justify herself in moral and spiritual terms that are in a tone strangely disjunct from her actual problem. She sees herself not simply as a woman fighting a rival, an act that needs little justification, but as an angel destroying the forces of evil; her ruthlessness is masked by conscious piety.

The effect of Maggie's movements in the latter half of the novel is terrifying. In the attempt to preserve what is most precious to her she becomes a vehicle of destruction and retribution that, in spite of appearances, have nothing to do with the just claims of outraged innocence. Yet she has those claims. And yet not altogether, not unambiguously, for she and her father have perpetrated things between them from the very beginning that are outrageous too. Even before Charlotte's marriage, Maggie and Adam have begun to settle into a new and deeper association, like a pair of cuckoos with the fruit of Amerigo's nest:

It was of course an old story and a familiar idea that a beautiful baby could take its place as a new link between a wife and a husband, but Maggie and her father had, with every ingenuity, converted the precious creature into a link between a mamma and a grandpapa. The Principino, for a chance spectator of this process, might have become, by an untoward stroke, a hapless half-orphan, with the place of the immediate male parent swept bare and open to the next nearest sympathy. (XXIII, 156)

Furthermore, Maggie and her father arrange Adam's marriage in a calculated effort to assuage Maggie's anxiety. He has "lost" something by her marriage. "What I feel is that there's somehow something that used to be right and that I've made wrong. It used to be right that you had n't married and that you did n't seem to want to" (XXIII, 171), she tells him. Worse, he is now open prey: "It was as if you could n't be in the market when you were married to *me*. Or rather as if I kept people off, innocently, by being married to you. Now that I'm married to some one else you're, as in consequence, married to nobody. Therefore you may be married to anybody, to everybody. People don't see why you should n't be married to *them*" (XXIII, 172). And so Adam decides he will marry Charlotte "for his child"; his motivation is "the measure of relief" that will be effected for her. Nor does this motivation escape Charlotte: it hardly can, he is quite explicit with her.

"To put her [Maggie] at peace is therefore," he explained, "what I'm trying, with you, to do. . . . You 'll effectively put out of her mind that I feel she has abandoned me. . . ."

". . . Isn't it, possibly," Charlotte asked, "not quite enough to marry me for? . . . Don't you appear rather to put it to me that I may accept your offer for Maggie's sake?" (XXIII, 223–224)

One of the real strokes here, and it is a phenomenon that operates all through *The Golden Bowl*, is the inextricable mixture of generosity and selfishness, of awareness and unawareness. What Maggie and her father are doing is outrageous only if viewed from a perspective other than their own. In terms of conscious purity of motive they are unimpeachable. Maggie wishes Adam to marry for his sake, he agrees to do so for hers. And the boldness of the language she uses—"when you were married to *me*"—attests to that conscious purity as nothing else could. The testimonial is in the very juxtaposition of the overt meaning of her words with their darker implications. If she were aware of the latter she could not speak the way she speaks. Yet the other perspective is unavoidable. The horror of this book—and its genius—is that it sustains a twofold vision to the very end and insists upon the interplay of diametrically opposed modes of understanding the same events. This "dream novel," as Ferner Nuhn has called it, contains a piece-by-piece—an inlay—nightmare. There are few events that are not susceptible of two interpretations; the duality is omnipresent and unrelenting. Two pairs of eyes see the events of this novel, and the effect of this double perspective is that we can take sides with no one. Or perhaps more accurately, we must take sides with everyone. The luxury of single identification is denied the reader; his pity and judgment must be spread over all the troubled human waters that come within the book's horizon.

The novel's structure is a further complication in what is already an extremely complex mode of seeing. James remarks in the Preface that his preference for dealing with his subject matter, for "seeing" his story "through the opportunity and the sensibility of some more or less detached, some not strictly involved, though thoroughly interested and intelligent, witness or reporter," [10] has been adhered to. The first half of the novel is (for the most part) a register of the Prince's consciousness of what is unfolding; the second half is a register of the Princess's consciousness. This does not mean, however, that we identify with Amerigo in the first part of the novel and with Maggie in the second: the process is considerably more complicated than that. If anything, the emotional effect is just the reverse, for the shift in perspective corresponds with a shift in control as well as in knowledge. In the first half Maggie is the passive, unwitting victim standing in the outer darkness and being practiced upon without knowing it. In the second half positions become gradually reversed until it is the Prince and Charlotte, especially Charlotte, who are the ones practiced upon, who are condemned to uncertainty and ignorance, and whose actions are groping, largely defensive, as the initiative passes from their hands into those of

[10] *The Art of the Novel: Critical Prefaces,* ed. R. P. Blackmur (New York, 1962), p. 327. Though limiting the point of view mainly to that of the major characters, James sometimes speaks in the ("implied") authorial voice—invoking at the same time an *imaginary* observer, in keeping with his preference for rendering reality through the medium of an attendant mind: "Adam Verver, at Fawns, that autumn Sunday might have been observed to open the door of the billiard-room with a certain freedom—might have been observed, that is, had there been a spectator in the field" (XXIII, 125). Though this phantom spectator is invoked only hypothetically, and then only to be dismissed, he has served his purpose: "This is how this scene would appear to an onlooker who is not the author." The *author* (or author as narrator) is privy *first of all* to what the phantom "would have" seen. The effect of the suggested presence of the latter lingers through the ensuing description even though narrator-James goes on to speak in his own person. Adam is entirely alone during the scene.

Maggie and her father. In each case the focus of pity is upon the person or persons in the gravest plight, the ones who are helpless in the face of manipulations they cannot control or even see very well.

But neither does this mean that we identify with Maggie in the first portion and the Prince and Charlotte in the second, because pity alone does not constitute the full association of oneself with a character that identification involves. The very fact of activity is an element in such an association, as is understanding, and as is judgment (the amount of justification we feel a given character has for the course of action he selects). That Maggie has an extraordinary amount is something we are never allowed to forget. But then, so do Charlotte and the Prince. What really happens is that first from one center of balance and then from another we are simultaneously given two views of the events as they occur. The two views are maintained all the way through the novel, regardless of where the "center of consciousness" happens to lie. At any given time one of these views is implicit, the other explicit: the explicit one is the subjective vision of the character whose state of consciousness is being recorded, the implicit one is "objective," with the character being seen (by other characters, by the reader) as well as seeing, being judged as well as judging.

This kind of complexity exists in any novel that is related from more than one "point of view." To some extent it exists in any novel related from the perspective of an observer [11] rather than that of the author. When such novels are concerned to present an unambiguous, "reliable" rendering of reality, the observer's word must

[11] Even if the "observer" is a major character.

be checked from a standpoint posited by the terms of the work as trustworthy: that of other, unbiased characters, or one deducible from evidence implicit in events. The full meaning of any such work is thus contingent upon sets of attitudes and communities of experience shared by author and reader in terms of which what is reported by the character is continually sifted, re-evaluated, and placed in a perspective which may be quite different from that of the reporter. In such instances, when one level of meaning contradicts or clashes with another and a "correct" response is predicated by the work, the writer and reader (or audience) are often secret bedfellows to the exclusion of the actors. Such communication both provides and posits a security where attitudes are rooted in general experience, giving a basis for proper understanding of the events, making their meaning intelligible.

But, as we have seen, some works—including many of James's—though they may rely heavily, for ironic reasons, upon traditional moral outlooks or modes of seeing and understanding life, do not presuppose a "correct" response (i.e. some final, objective truth) when they present contradictory or clashing viewpoints. All that is required for "intelligibility" in such works is the coherence of each separate view or "fiction." Sometimes the interest of such works resides in the collision of the fictions—that is, in the ironic encounter of different subjective universes, precisely in their clash; sometimes it resides more in the analogues the process of "meaning-making" provides—in parody or in celebration—for creativity in general; or, in extreme forms in certain contemporary works, with the conscious insistence upon their own fictionality, in the deliberate, mocking breakdown of responses commonly appropriate to "art" on the one hand and "life" on the other.

Maggie, in *The Golden Bowl*, sees herself again and again as an actress improvising a whole new role, inventing from moment to moment what to say and do, with her friends as figures "rehearsing some play of which she herself was the author": in short, she sees herself as the conscious creator of her own universe, demanding only of herself "ideal consistency." But to accomplish the latter, James tells us, "she had always been capable of cutting down more or less her prior term" (XXIV, 6); in other words of altering the postulates upon which the coherency of her world rests, creating, like the narrator in *The Sacred Fount*, a series of closed systems, hypothetical models. One difference between that narrator and Maggie is that Maggie's structures are not meant to be simply *interpretations* of the reality around her but also *models of action*, to be imposed upon the people around her. And she does indeed become author of their universe. The only "rule" her fictions must obey (apart from internal consistency) is that appearances, though they may be manipulated, must be preserved.

This image of herself as creator makes explicit and has its analogues in the characteristic mode of rendering reality throughout the novel, which is, as we have indicated, the objectification of the consciousnesses of the (principal) narrators by means of elaborate extended metaphors: images—really almost metaphysical conceits—for their apprehension of the world and their own relation to it. These images—prolonged, intensely vivid—create a dreamlike tapestry of other figures and places (other than the "actual" ones in the book) that form a continuous backdrop, a ghostly reflection of the reality in the novel; the novel is, literally, "haunted."

Another difference between Maggie and the narrator of *The Sacred Fount* is that the latter's consciousness is self-consuming and never at any point "verified" in the course of the novel, while Maggie's is not only verified and not only put forth as a model of action, but, as such, is efficacious. It objectively alters, literally recreates, the conditions and hence the nature of what is around her. Both characters are conceived of as demonic figures, but the narrator of the earlier book is an impotent demon whose spells don't work. Maggie's work but, as in all Satanic magic, to the ultimate grief of both practitioner and victim.

In the figure of Maggie, creator and destroyer become one—a notion that is inherent in the concept of "creator" anyhow: who has power to make has power to annihilate. First, she arranged the marriage of her father and stepmother, thus bringing into being the situation she is soon to react to. Then, when she becomes aware of the ensuing adultery, she puts into effect a program that shatters the happiness and irrevocably changes the lives of all four of the principal characters. The destruction of their joy is not postulated as her intent (except possibly with respect to Charlotte), but it is seen, objectively, as the effect of her actions. But James is demonic too. The only alternatives he allows Maggie under the burden of her knowledge once it is a fact are to suffer the adultery of her husband and stepmother in silence (i.e., to remain a passive and helpless victim); to proclaim her knowledge and cause the public collapse of what dignity remains to them all through the preservation of social form, abiding by "the rules of the game"; or to manipulate reality while preserving appearances, thus turning the tables on Charlotte and Amerigo, making them the helpless victims and herself demonic. To be destroyed, to destroy openly, to destroy covertly: not a very pretty set of alternatives.

What Maggie as "author" does to herself and the three people closest to her is analogous to what James "does" to the same characters: he brought them into conjunction, determined their conditions, and then ravaged them, wielding the artist's prerogative over the life and death of his fictional universe. In a certain sense the novel thus addresses itself to the exploration and representation of the creative process itself. We are shown the controlling consciousness in each part of the book concretizing itself in metaphor, "realizing" itself by means of the imaginary. This consciousness creates and manipulates appearances (and it is these alone with which an author deals—fictions, in the Platonic sense "lies") of terrible beauty, extraordinary artistry, and confronts us with an ironic juxtaposition of the beauty of these appearances and their ".truth." [12] What seems to be is *not* the case; precisely the opposite is:

[12] This depiction of a consciousness penetrating some veil to the truth "hideously behind" it in some intuitive divination of a principle of evil in the universe is a very *American* kind of perception. To establish and then be undone by a *moral* discrepancy between appearance and reality; to insist with that extraordinary American "good faith," as the Prince says of Maggie, on one's own and everybody else's essential benignity until the shock of recognition strikes home is a typical dualism in American art. This process of first equating and then severing phenomena and noumena comes to be identified with a movement from a false consciousness of good to a "true" consciousness of evil. Whitman, poet of "radical good," represents only the first stage of this process,

The Negative Imagination

She saw at all events why horror itself had almost failed her . . . the horror of finding evil seated all at its ease where she had only dreamed of good; the horror of the thing hideously *behind,* behind so much trusted, so much pretended, nobleness, cleverness, tenderness. It was the first sharp falsity she had known in her life, to touch at all or be touched by; it had met her like some bad-faced stranger surprised in one of the thick-carpeted corridors of a house of quiet on a Sunday afternoon. (XXIV, 237)

Finally, the controlling center of perception creates a new relation between appearance and reality by means of which, in this case, it wreaks destruction. All of these processes represent aspects and possible implications of the creative consciousness, the concretization of which is James's concern in *The Golden Bowl.*

In the creation and comprehension of her world, Maggie uses concepts from traditional moral experience:

---

his poetry remaining frozen in its "complete identification with the beauty of appearances." Poe (appropriately in this sense the mentor of Baudelaire) represents only the second stage, concerned as he is less with the movement *to* the "true" consciousness of evil than with taking it as a given and depicting its extremity and excruciation with detail, subtlety, refinement. But Melville, Hawthorne, and James are concerned with the dynamics of this shift in apprehension. James's novels are always in the business of surprising that bad-faced stranger in a peaceful house on Sunday. To postulate a morally neutral "reality"—whatever its relation to appearance—or to *un*naïvely equate essence and appearance, as Robbe-Grillet would do, is not characteristic of American fiction. Roquentin, in Sartre's *Nausea,* also addresses himself to the relation between the way things seem and the way they really are, or between existence as our perception disguises it and existence naked, revealed. But though existence revealed "nauseates" Roquentin, it is a perceptual and spiritual, not a *moral,* nausea he experiences.

"right," "evil," and so on—indeed she has to see herself (though occasionally she acknowledges motives of expediency) as largely justified in terms of this way of categorizing human life. But, as we shall discover, the only way she is able to do so is precisely by "cutting down her prior term"—creating new assumptions, redefining, in a process of continuous creation, her moral universe to the point where "good" and "evil" ultimately become indistinguishable.

In spite of these complexities and those of the narrative method, *The Golden Bowl* has an astonishing kind of lucidity, luminosity, and rigor of logic. It is neither incoherent nor muddy; its insanity is beautifully rational, like an intricate mathematical proof correct in every detail except for the assumption upon which it is based. Moreover, as we have said, the events are clear enough, the action is well defined, there is a definite, describable "story." The ambiguity in the novel is a function of the dizzying alterations in the moral assumptions, the shifting worlds created from them.

It is important to keep this in mind, because the change in narrative point of view alone creates a complex emotional effect that makes the demands upon the inner resources of the reader considerable indeed. In the simplest terms, we are required to share the inner worlds of two people [13] who are at odds with each other at the same time that their lives are mutually dependent. "It is the Prince who opens the door to half our light upon Maggie, just as it is she who opens it to half our light

[13] We are also given, especially in Book I, glimpses into Adam and Fanny. James refers to this "disparity" as superficial, since they are only glimpses.

upon himself.[14] Each character is presented as seen by himself and as seen by the other. The reader is condemned to share both visions of both people. And since their relation, in spite of all its pulls and ties, protections and adorations, guardings of appearance and care taken not to wound openly, is essentially unloving, the reader's post of observation cannot help but be uncomfortable. We are asked to understand almost too much: both the persons who do the hurting and those who are hurt. And since these roles, in turn, are gradually reversed in the course of events, the reader must extend himself even further.

So that even if James's moral intention with respect to Maggie were unambiguous, the narrative method would still enforce a division of our sympathies. I think there can be no doubt that James both knew this and intended it. It was he who made the use of "point of view" a theoretical cornerstone for the art of fiction, and his preoccupation with the particular effects achievable by utilizing a central intelligence as a compositional focus is well known. Further, his only comments in the Preface to *The Golden Bowl* that are actually devoted to the novel itself concern just this subject. He disavows "the mere muffled majesty of irresponsible 'authorship'" as opposed to his ideal of seeing his story through someone's eyes, and says that although authorship *"ostensibly"* may reign in the novel, "I catch myself again shaking it off . . . while I get down into the arena and do my best to live and breathe and rub shoulders and converse with the persons engaged in the struggle that provides for the others in the circling tiers the entertainment of the great game. There

[14] *The Art of the Novel,* p. 330.

is no other participant, of course, than each of the real, the deeply involved and immersed and more or less bleeding participants." The language alone here makes quite clear his awareness of the inevitable division of our feelings among these "bleeding participants." There is certainly no indication that his intent was to limit our identification to Maggie's plight alone. If anything, indications are to the contrary. The Prince's consciousness in the first half, a consciousness "highly susceptible of registration," is a kind of mirror or "clean glass," James says, "and yet after all never a whit to the prejudice of his being *just as consistently a foredoomed, entangled, embarrassed agent in the general imbroglio, actor in the offered play. The function of the Princess, in the remainder, matches exactly with his*" (italics mine).[15]

An approach to the novel that does not take this narrative method into account is bound to run into difficulties. Leavis, for example, dismisses the book as "morally unsatisfactory" on the grounds that our sympathies lie where they aren't supposed to: with the adulterers.

"James clearly counts," Leavis writes, "on our taking towards his main persons [Maggie and her father] attitudes that we cannot take without forgetting our finer moral sense—our finer discriminative feeling for life and personality." He explains that Adam and Maggie "collect" the Prince in the same spirit in which they collect their other "pieces," and that James is explicit about this.

And yet, though James can on occasion come to this point of explicitness, our attitude toward the Ververs isn't meant to be ironical. We are to feel for and with them. We are to watch

---

[15] *The Art of the Novel*, pp. 328–329.

with intense sympathy Maggie's victorious struggle to break the clandestine relation between her husband and Charlotte. . . . Actually, if our sympathies are anywhere they are with Charlotte and (a little) the Prince, who represent what, against the general moral background of the book can only strike us as decent passion.[16]

The assumption here is that the novel presents one autonomous vision that should elicit a clearly defined set of responses in which our sympathy and judgment are not at odds. Yet according to the Preface, James's conception of the effects he had achieved by his narrative approach was considerably more complicated than Leavis suggests.

First of all, the Preface makes clear how James savored his technical achievement in maintaining such perfect balance and formal opposition between the two books of the novel: an achievement that introduces us into the consciousnesses of *each* of the two embattled protagonists and by that very act creates a division in our response. He speaks with pride of the way the "thing abides rigidly by its law of showing Maggie Verver at first through her suitor's and her husband's exhibitory vision of her, and then of showing the Prince, with at least an equal intensity, through his wife's."[17] He celebrates the "endless interest, endless worth for 'delight,' of the compositional contribution"[18] made by the fortune of the "admirably endowed pair" and by his own method of presenting them. The choreography of the book fascinated him: he wanted to squeeze every drop of dramatic and ironic effect possible through "placing" his figures in

[16] F. R. Leavis, *The Great Tradition* (Garden City, New York, 1954), pp. 194–195.

[17] *The Art of the Novel,* p. 330.   [18] *Ibid.,* p. 329.

parallel and contrasting positions. In *The Destructive Element*, Stephen Spender gives us a kind of algebraic representation of the groupings and regroupings of the four major characters that shows very vividly the intricate symmetry James achieved in the plot.[19] The remarks in the Preface are in fact limited to the architectonics of the novel and to the enchanting possibilities James saw in them:

We see very few persons in "The Golden Bowl," but the scheme of the book, to make up for that, is that we really see about as much of them as a coherent literary form permits. That was my problem, so to speak, and my *gageure*—to play the small handful of values really for all they were worth—and to work my system, my particular propriety of appeal, particular degree of pressure on the spring of interest, for all that this specific ingenuity itself might be.[20]

Second, as his remark about his "bleeding participants" indicates, in telling his story by this process of double refraction, James seems to have been moved by a complex impulse to show his awareness of the endless interlinking chain of human guilt and grief and love, to see life through what he calls in the novel "the dim window of human trouble in general" and to render the responsibility, suffering, and helplessness of all his major actors. These were certainly the effects he sought in *The Wings of the Dove,* until his somewhat too glib ending undercut them, and also in *The Ambassadors.* The whole burden of Strether's experience, as we have seen, showed the insufficiency of a legalistic and overly rigid concept of human sin. The fault of *The Wings of the Dove* is that

[19] (London, 1935), pp. 87–88.
[20] *The Art of the Novel,* pp. 330–331.

such a concept is allowed to dictate the closing movements of the book, but the book itself fortunately has
enough passion and strength of insight to survive these
final manipulations. So that it is difficult to believe James
would resort, for the premise of his last work, to a
conception he had written a whole novel (*The Ambassadors*) to disprove. Yet this is the assumption held by
Leavis, Blackmur, and others: that James meant us to see
that Maggie was "right" and Amerigo and Charlotte were
"wrong." This notion is contradicted by the language of
the Preface, by the general tenor of the immediately
preceding works, and by numerous actual effects in the
novel itself. Charlotte's grief and terror, for example, at
the end are very real, are in no sense incidental or
ignored. Maggie herself weeps at Charlotte's anguish, and
the language used to describe that anguish (the "quaver"
of her voice is "like the shriek of a soul in pain") could
hardly be more explicit.

There is in fact *no* indication that James did not intend
us to have compassion for Charlotte, however problemati-
cally she is seen (the rendering of Maggie is in fact
infinitely more problematic). Even with its ambiguities,
this novel, like the others, is a many-faceted exploration of
inner human nature, of the paradoxical relationship
between desire and destruction, which James sees as a
fundamental aspect of our existence.

His approach to morality is, as always, in terms of this
paradox: Leavis would have to look far in James to find
the genuinely golden, disinterested, selfless hero or
heroine he regrets the Ververs are not. Strether and even
Milly have needs that make them relinquish their own
human status to become objects in the game of others,

and both in turn dehumanize, though in a passive way, the most important people in their environment in order to make a wish come true. Chad and Madame de Vionnet represent for Strether his lost youth, at once chaste and sexual; Merton represents for Milly her chance for life. In the face of these needs the other possible commitments and passions of their friends are ignored, undone, obliterated by this innocent pair.

The essential perceptions are the same in all three novels; *The Golden Bowl* pursues their implications further and more ambiguously than the other two books, but the difference is one of degree not kind. Morality is seen in each book as a necessary system of sanctions whose function is to curb the blind longings and uncontrolled desires of the individual. It is "necessary" because without it only destruction and pain ensue, but it is no bringer of happiness. The alternative to the total consummation of their wishes is for all of the characters, "good" and "bad" alike, a meaningless compromise, half a life, or even, as in Milly's case, none at all. All of the characters consistently reject this alternative, and it is out of this rejection that the basic dramatic situation of the novels springs.

So too with *The Golden Bowl:* the irreconcilable nature of the conflict does not come just from the fact that the new *sposi* of Adam and Maggie Verver were once lovers, ripe though such a situation potentially is. Nor does it even come from the fact that these same *sposi* married into the Verver menage for money and security and power rather than love. The conflict develops out of the unwillingness of all the parties concerned to give up anything in exchange for the new *status quo*, or to

187

compromise their deepest wishes, even if they are contradictory, and be content with the good they have. Maggie wants to have her husband totally without giving up an inch of her father:

The pagoda in her blooming garden figured the arrangement —how otherwise was it to be named?—by which, so strikingly, she had been able to marry without breaking, as she liked to put it, with her past. She had surrendered herself to her husband without the shadow of a reserve or a condition and yet had n't all the while given up her father by the least little inch. . . . What had moreover all the while enriched the whole aspect of success was that the latter's marriage had been no more measurably paid for than her own. His having taken the same great step in the same free way had n't in the least involved the relegation of his daughter. (XXIV, 5)

And Amerigo and Charlotte in their turn want the material and social benefits their marriages have purchased for them without giving each other up. This is the case of course in spite of the pure intentions and good faith with which the Prince at least entered his marriage contract. (Charlotte's "intentions" are slightly cloudier.) For in the face of the intensity of their sexual passion, the permission he gives Charlotte to marry Adam can only rightly be read one way. At the best, it is a case of the right hand not letting the left hand know what it is up to, and at any rate even that degree of unawareness does not last:

He knew why he had from the first of his marriage [21] tried with such patience for such conformity; he knew why he had given up so much and bored himself so much; he knew why he

[21] This too is indicative, because Amerigo and Maggie had been married for some time before Charlotte weds Adam.

had at any rate gone in, on the basis of all forms, on the basis of his having in a manner sold himself, for a *situation nette*. It had all been just in order that his—well, what on earth should he call it but his freedom?—should at present be as perfect and rounded and lustrous as some huge precious pearl. He had n't struggled nor snatched; he was taking but what had been given him; the pearl dropped itself, with its exquisite quality and rarity, straight into his hand. Here precisely it was, incarnate; its size and its value grew as Mrs. Verver appeared, afar off, in one of the smaller doorways. She came toward him. . . .

"I feel the day like a great gold cup that we must somehow drain together." (XXIII, 358–359)

Like Milly, these four survey their respective "kingdoms of the earth" not so much to choose among them as to have them all; like Kate and like Strether they repudiate the very idea of having to make a "choice" but assert by their actions that it somehow must be, somehow is, possible to have the best of all worlds. But the selection of goods is limited: "One beautiful woman and one beautiful fortune," Fanny insists when her husband asks why after all the Prince needs two beautiful women. The cleavage is sharp, as it was with Milly and Kate Croy. Milly has "a high dim charming ambiguous oddity" but "not beauty," and though the former qualities are "even better" (XIX, 110) to Susan Stringham, they are not to the males hovering about. Kate on the contrary, "slender and simple, frequently soundless . . . was somehow always in the line of the eye—she counted singularly for its pleasure." The same point of comparative drabness is made with respect to Maggie: "She had ever been, in respect to her clothes, rather timorous and uncertain; for the last year above all she had lived in the light of Charlotte's possible and rather inscrutable judgment of them. Charlotte's own were simply the most charming and interesting any woman had ever put on" (XXIV, 13).

The essential elements out of which the conflict springs thus are much the same in the three novels. The internal clash arises from the either-or quality of the possibilities for happiness that face each character: either I can have a rich, acceptable, boring wife or a poor, outcast, sexually exciting wife; either I can satisfy the dictates of my conscience and of society or I can quench my sensual and aesthetic appetites. The external clash, or struggle between the characters, results from their unwillingness to resolve the internal conflict. The result is that the characters become rivals instead of friends, and the relationship between them becomes hostile, competitive, inevitably destructive. But the novels are by no means treatises on the necessity for control and compromise: they are more like troubled sighs of regret that man as a social animal is doomed at best to dissatisfaction and frustration or, if he won't take *that* fate lying down or stoically (and the Jamesian character won't; in this sense he is the antithesis of the Faulkner Negro, whose strength is in his capacity to "endure" the impoverishments and vicissitudes of life), he finds himself as a consequence in a relation of unending pain and hurt with his fellow creatures.

In all of these respects *The Golden Bowl* closely parallels its two predecessors and most of the earlier works as well. The nature and form of the conflict are the same, as are the theme of sexual rivalry and the division of the characters into two fundamental polar types, the worldly and the innocent. This polarity is introduced in the first chapter: the drops with which Maggie sweetens the Prince's golden waters "were of the colour—of what on earth? of what but the extraordinary American good faith? They were of the colour of her innocence, and yet at the same time of her imagination, with which their relation, his and these people's was all suffused. . . . 'You Americans [he says] are almost incredibly romantic'" (XXIII, 10–11). Contrasting this color of innocence is the Prince's heritage, "made up of the history, the doings, the marriages, the crimes, the follies, the boundless *bêtises* of other people," things that "are as public as they're abominable" (XXIII, 9).

One of the ways that *The Golden Bowl* most differs from its predecessors is in the exploration of the changing relationship between these two types. This exploration in turn is based upon the most problematic search into the darker aspects of the psyche that is to be found in James's fiction. This can be most clearly seen in the figure of Maggie, who takes her place in the long roll of vulnerable innocents who people the novels: Hyacinth Robinson, Catherine Sloper, Daisy Miller, Nanda Brooks, Isabel Archer, Milly Theale, Lambert Strether. Like all of them, Maggie is practiced upon, manipulated, deceived, betrayed, and victimized by the very people who are closest to her and whom she most needs to trust and love. But she is the only one in this list who fights back in an extraordinary effort to reassert control over her own destiny. The second half of the novel is precisely a study of her counterreaction, her transition from a helpless, obliging passivity to a determined resistance and calculated aggression. The hint of this comes first at the end of Book I when Fanny says, "I like the idea of Maggie audacious and impudent—learning to be so to gloss things over. She could—she even will, yet, I believe— learn it, for that sacred purpose,[22] consummately, diabolically" (XXIII, 396–397).

And we watch Maggie learn her diabolical art from moment to moment under the pressure of first anxiety, then overt suspicion, and finally certain knowledge. Essentially it is the art of manipulating appearances; she has had good teachers in her husband and his mistress, but even so she is impressively adept for someone whose imagination has been sealed to evil and who has been "the creature in the world to whom a wrong thing could least be communicated" (XXIII, 384). This is the paradox that lies at the center of *The Golden Bowl*: the capacity for guile and darkness in the person least acquainted with them, the tiger in the lamb. Maggie's practical victory is very real. But to achieve it she manipulates, lies, and twists all advantages to her purpose regardless of who suffers, or how much he suffers. Ferner Nuhn suggests that if the book had been written from Charlotte's point of view, Maggie would turn out to be the "bad witch" instead of the "lovely Princess of the fairy tale." [23] But, as we have indicated, the novel is sufficiently sympathetic to Charlotte so that this darker image of Maggie emerges anyhow. She is called "deep," "terrible," "diabolic" by her husband and Fanny. A careful reading of the ending of

[22] The purpose is to keep her father unconscious of what is happening.
[23] *The Wind Blew from the East: A Study in the Orientation of American Culture* (New York, 1940), p. 133.

the book does not *in any way* substantiate the idea of moral triumph; the note is one of tragic fear and dread, not spiritual exultation. There is no indication that Amerigo has come to love her better than he did in the beginning, or indeed at all. What he does admit is that he underestimated her, that she is a much more formidable person than he had imagined at first. In *The Wings of the Dove*, by contrast, Densher's change of *heart* is made explicit: "You're in love with her memory," Kate tells him, and he does not deny it. Nor is it ever suggested that anything "beautiful" or "exquisite" has happened to Amerigo as he becomes aware of the kind of woman his wife is. Rather, he becomes "a proud man reduced to abjection" (XXIV, 228) and "mystified, confounded, tormented" (XXIV, 135), as Fanny predicts.

James has always intuited a connection between predator and victim; in itself this was an early perception of his, and forms the basis for many of his works in addition to *The Ambassadors* and *The Wings of the Dove*. But in Maggie we have for the first time their fusion in the same person, and she is the major symbol for what the Prince in his worldly bewilderment troubles and puzzles over in the social scene around him: "the element of staleness in all the freshness and of freshness in all the staleness, of innocence in the guilt and of guilt in the innocence" (XXIII, 354). It is the mixture of course that confuses the Prince, not the phenomena in and of themselves. He has an automatic expectation of wickedness in his fellow men, and his formula for human behavior is that most men act from self-interest, but that there are a few incredible romantics like his wife—perhaps like Americans in general—or like Fanny Assingham, who act from no such motive, who are or seem strangely selfless. It is not in the medium of evil that the Prince finds himself at sea, but rather in "the fathomless depths of English equivocation" (XXIII, 353). He is uncomfortable when he cannot see clearly what someone has to gain from an action or when what they have to gain is clouded by other issues. Why does Fanny Assingham help him so much? Why does his wife-to-be invest him with attributes? The Prince does not know: "These things, the motives of such people, were obscure—a little alarmingly so; they contributed to that element of the impenetrable which alone slightly qualified his sense of his good fortune." He recalls Poe's tale of the shipwrecked Gordon Pym,

who, drifting in a small boat further toward the North Pole—or was it the South?—than any one had ever done, found at a given moment before him a thickness of white air that was like a dazzling curtain of light, concealing as darkness conceals, yet of the colour of milk or of snow. There were moments when he felt his own boat move upon some such mystery. The state of mind of his new friends, including Mrs. Assingham herself, had resemblances to a great white curtain. He had never known curtains but as purple even to blackness—but as producing where they hung a darkness intended and ominous. (XXIII, 22–23)

The thing about a white curtain that makes it so terrifying is that it is a double mask: like the black one it hides what is behind it, but unlike the black one it suggests that what is hidden must be benign—yet that of course cannot be the case, else why is it hidden? The image suggests Melville's chapter "the Whiteness of the Whale," in which he tries to explain why it was above all things the color of Moby Dick that appalled Ishmael. He traces some of its spiritual associations, and then remarks, "Yet for all these accumulated associations, with whatever is sweet, and honorable, and sublime, there yet lurks an elusive something in the innermost idea of this hue which strikes more of panic to the soul than that redness which affrights in blood."

Why? He gives two partial answers, the first having to do with an unholy contrast, the linking together of violently opposed associations. Perhaps, some would say, the polar bear's "heightened hideousness" is due to the circumstance that "the irresponsible ferociousness of the creature stands invested in the fleece of celestial innocence and love; and hence, by bringing together two such opposite emotions in our minds, the Polar bear frightens us with so unnatural a contrast." The very contrast between a sign that "is at once the most meaning symbol of spiritual things, nay, the very veil of the Christian's Deity; and yet . . . is the intensifying agent in things most appalling to mankind" suggests that though "in many of its aspects this visible world seems formed in love, the invisible spheres were formed in fright."

Yet, for all that, "if it were not for the whiteness, you would not have the intensified terror"; so there is something about the color itself evocative of horror. In its physical nature it is at once the "visible absence of color, and at the same time the concrete of all colors" and has a kind of indefiniteness to the senses that "shadows forth the heartless voids and immensities of the universe, and thus stabs us from behind with the thought of annihilation, when beholding the white depths of the milky way." Perhaps it is for these reasons that there is such a "dumb blankness, full of meaning, in a wide landscape of snows—a colorless, all-color of atheism from which we shrink." This then is part of the horror: the suggestive blankness.

But the blankness and dread of annihilation are only part of the answer, for the very notion of color—"the sweet tinges of sunset . . . the butterfly cheeks of young girls . . . are but subtile deceits, not actually inherent in substances, but only laid on from without; so that all deified Nature absolutely paints like the harlot, whose allurements cover nothing but the charnel-house within"; indeed, the great principle of light itself "if operating without medium upon matter, would touch all objects, even tulips and roses, with its own blank tinge—pondering all this, the palsied universe lies before us as a leper; and . . . the wretched infidel gazes himself blind at the monumental white shroud that wraps all the prospect around him." [24] The terror then is not only the thought of personal death, but of some disguised principle of decay and sickness and paralysis at the very center of the universe.

The Prince knows, to his bewilderment, that he is "taken seriously," and that "lost there in the white mist" of the disguised and obscure motives of his friends "was the seriousness in *them* that made them so take him" (XXIII, 23–24). It is bewildering because to anyone of his own ken his motivations would be instantly apparent; *he* is at a loss to understand anyone who does not understand him. And the metaphor of the voyage is pursued as he pleads with Fanny not to abandon him, but to stay by him and

[24] Herman Melville, *Moby-Dick: Or the Whale* (New York, 1953), pp. 184–192.

help him to see: "I'm starting on the great voyage—across the unknown sea; my ship's all rigged and appointed. . . . But what seems the matter with me is that I can't sail alone. . . . I must keep your sail in sight for orientation" (XXIII, 26). Otherwise, he won't know where he is:

"No—with you people it 's a sense. We have n't got it—not as you have. Therefore—!" . . .

"I should be interested," she presently remarked, "to see some sense *you* don't possess."

Well, he produced one on the spot. "The moral, dear Mrs. Assingham." (XXIII, 30–31)

And here we reach the basic opposition in the novel, the struggle between two clashing orientations toward life, two basic sets of attitudes controlling the responses and behavior of the individuals who hold them. In a real sense the portraits of these orientations are historical. The Prince has no particular personal or innate incapacity for moral awareness; rather, he is the product and distillation of his culture, "dear backward old Rome," whose moral sense, he tells Fanny, is no more like that of the English (or American) race "than the tortuous stone staircase— half-ruined into the bargain!—in some castle of our *quattrocento* is like the 'lightning elevator' in one of Mr. Verver's fifteen-storey buildings. Your moral sense works by steam—it sends you up like a rocket. Ours is slow and steep and unlighted, with so many of the steps missing that—well, that it 's as short in almost any case to turn round and come down again" (XXIII, 30–31). The contrast is of course once again between the Old World and the New, weary Europe and modern America, and the term "historical" must be understood in the light of these symbolic structures that James consistently uses to organize reality, and that are intuitive in nature rather than discursive. He is not concerned with the "past" as a sequence of causally related, politically significant events cast in the framework of a struggle for survival or power, but rather as the medium through which the burden of human culture is accumulated and transmitted, and as a context for the preservation of the unregenerate human conscience. It is true that he vaguely connects the latter with "follies and crimes, waste and plunder" and "the wicked Pope," but which crimes and plunder, even which wicked Pope, is not specified, nor needs to be. The Prince is one with his bad Pope; both are timeless and the very vagueness is just the point. It is the phenomenon itself of a predatory relation to other human beings—of waste and wickedness erected into a style of life—which is of concern, not the particular representatives of that style.

Amerigo and Maggie are both seen historically, in the sense that they are the finest flowers of their respective civilizations. In a way they are denied personality, for each functions as the embodiment of the complex pattern of traits, stances, and attitudes that James sees as characteristically "European" or characteristically "American." It would be difficult if not impossible to describe either actor in terms that did not refer to his cultural origins, and even the Prince's insistence upon his unknown "single self" and "personal quantity," which exist apart from his "history," is an inverted ironic illusion. For what he is doing is warning his bride-to-be that there is more to him than meets the eye, that there are certain situations he would not hesitate to exploit for his personal advantage. Yet the fact that she is his bride-to-be is such a situation; and the one story his history tells over and over is just the holy quest for personal gain.

But the concern in the novel with the two opposing civilizations is very much a private concern, in that what finally matters is the possibilities for personal happiness represented by each. And one of the things that happen is that under the pressure of individual need, hunger, and pain, both systems crumble, both "styles of life" collapse; the boundaries and barriers between them give way and they are shown, finally, to be more alike than different after all. Certainly they are alike in their inability to bear the burden of private anguish or to sustain their respective ambassadors in the foreignness of that burden.

And perhaps they resemble each other in other respects too. Unlike himself, the Prince's friends possess, he feels, a moral sense. And here we have of course the essential distinction James makes between Europe and America: that America has incorporated into her way of life an unshakable beatitude of conscience.

The form and inner workings of the American conscience, with its "odious ascetic suspicion of beauty," are delineated in much more detail in *The Ambassadors* than in *The Golden Bowl*,[25] in which it is more of a luminous and somewhat fuzzy halo hovering over Maggie and her father than a set of very clearly articulated particulars of manners and morals. But the essence, the oil of innocence so to speak, is very much there:

[The Prince to Maggie]
"You Americans are almost incredibly romantic."

[25] Such a difference is not surprising between a novel of manners and a "dream novel."

"Of course we are. That 's just what makes everything so nice for us."

"Everything?" He had wondered.

"Well, everything that 's nice at all. The world, the beautiful world—or everything in it that *is* beautiful. I mean we see so much." (XXIII, 11)

And so long as Maggie's dream of ubiquitous niceness remains unthreatened, her halo remains in place, but when the shadow falls on her marriage and she ceases to take comfort in its felicity, she finds herself held by a strange reluctance to ask why, a reluctance that "represented . . . a lapse from that ideal consistency on which her moral comfort almost at any time depended" (XXIV, 6).

With the birth of doubt in the validity of her own logic, Maggie's halo begins to waver. In a way, everything that she initiates from this point on can be looked at as an effort to re-establish consistency so that she may fight her dilemma without sacrificing the illusion of moral poise. And so she begins recasting the terms of her understanding [26] of the little Verver menage in a way that allows her flexibility of action without shattering the image of her own essential rectitude and profound innocence. It is a diabolic combination, for, really sustained, it is probably

[26] Her first step, for example, is to "participate" more in the experiences of her husband and stepmother. "What if I've abandoned *them*, you know? What if I've accepted too passively the funny form of our life?" (XXIV, 25) This assumption becomes the logical basis for her new position but does not constitute a real act of self-perception, in the sense that she does not recognize the implications of the kind of relation she and her father have maintained. And the notion that she has previously been too "passive" is in effect more self-congratulatory—for passivity is a "feminine" virtue—than anything else.

the nearest thing to psychic invulnerability that can be achieved, and under its guise any action, however destructive, may be justified.

What above all allows her to sustain her autonomous self-image is her awareness that she has been wronged. And however one may react to her ersatz piety, this awareness places her permanently beyond any easy judgment or pious dismissal on our own parts: we are not allowed to forget her very real pain or plight or stature. Yet under the warrant of that pain she engages in acts of conscious duplicity and manipulation that also place her far beyond simple pity. Confessing finally to Fanny that she is jealous, unhappy, tormented, Maggie says that she has sent the two lovers off on a weekend together, to see whether they *would,* now that they know that Maggie has been taking more notice of the "queer things in all their lives." And indeed, she explains, they had to go, though they certainly would much rather have not, lest their very avoidance of what they used to do automatically be grounds in itself for suspicion.

> "And that's how I make them do what I like!"
> It had an effect on Mrs. Assingham. . . . "My dear child, you're amazing."
> "Amazing—?"
> "You're terrible."
> Maggie thoughtfully shook her head. "No; I'm not terrible . . . but surprisingly mild. . . ."
> Mrs. Assingham, more brightly again, bridled. "Is that what you call it when you make them, for terror as you say, do as you like?"
> "Ah, there would n't be any terror for them if they had nothing to hide." (XXIV, 115–116)

So Gabriel might speak at the sounding of the trumpet.

They do of course have something to hide, and Maggie does rather resemble a conscious avenging angel in the second half of the novel, which is a study in the complicated tensions arising between their wrong and her response to it. Very quickly, however, we are involved in ambiguities concerning both the response, with its wavering and uncertain territory between justified and merely gratuitous retaliation, and the wrong, with its double face of her betrayed trust and their helpless passion. It is a kind of labyrinth in which each side has its own absolute claims until those claims are viewed from the perspective of the persons at whose expense they are made. When that happens the picture changes, and yet at the same time does not change. It is as if we are being asked both to regard whatever Maggie does in the face of her betrayal as "justified" and to see that everything she does do, in the final analysis, merely adds to the common burden of terror and woe, if only for the reason that whom one is supposed to love means next to nothing in the face of whom one does love.

Or to put it another way, the language of "I ought" is apt to flicker and pale beside that of "I want" or "I need." In this sense, not outraged innocence but passion justifies Maggie; but also then Charlotte and the Prince too. And up to a point this is exactly the case and we are asked to see the novel in terms of the institution of the triangle, which, with its two persons both hungering for the same third one, by definition entails suffering, mostly blameless suffering. But it is only up to a point that this applies, for the characters are moved by considerations other than those of sexual love. The beautiful fortune speaks louder to the Prince in the end than the beautiful woman, for example, and Adam removes to American City not to keep his wife but to help his daughter keep her husband. But it is above all with Maggie, moving with quiet determination from behind her white curtain, that the darkest ambiguities arise.

This perhaps can most easily be seen by asking what happens to her official American innocence and that "moral sense" which constitutes the main difference between her sensibility and that of her husband. One form her innocence takes is an ignorance of the distinction between reality and appearance, and this is appropriate enough since awareness of that distinction is part of what is meant by "knowledge" of good and evil.

The Prince's concern is with the world of appearances; the holy vow he and Charlotte take, never to "consciously wound," is a vow on the altar of that world. What is required of them is the preservation of the forms and rituals of constancy, the flawless mask, the terms of expediency. This accomplished, the "truth" cannot hurt anyone. For Maggie, however, in the beginning ritual and fact are one and the world *is* beautiful because she takes it at face value and so taking it she is indeed the apotheosis of innocence.

But once wrong is communicated to her and the hidden flaw in the golden bowl of her happiness becomes perceptible, a transformation takes place in Maggie, for then "we're talking," as Fanny so wisely knows, "of good innocent people deeply worked upon by a horrid discovery and going much further in their view of the lurid, as such people almost always do, than those who have been wider awake all round from the first. . . . No imagination's so lively, once it's started, as that of really agitated lambs. Lions are nothing to them, for lions are sophisticated, are *blasés*, are brought up from the first to prowling and mauling" (XXIV, 127–128).

The change in Maggie is not only in the intensity of her imagination, however, but in the total sense of her connection to reality. Essentially this involves the creation for the first time in her life of an "other," a public Maggie, consciously different from the private, the now secret Maggie. She joins her husband and stepmother in the deliberate manipulation of the world of appearances, learning, in her own words, "almost from minute to minute, to be a mistress of shades" (XXIV, 142). And the mask she dons for these public encounters is the ghost of her old, now permanently vanished self: humble Maggie, sweet Maggie, unsuspecting, oblivious Maggie—slightly more eager and ardent perhaps, as if she has felt left out of all the exciting things going on and would like now to be included—but at heart the same tender Maggie. Like them she operates now under the dictates of expediency and necessity, not morality, and the ensuing events resemble a chess game played by the most civilized of people for the most unholy of stakes. Under the polished and unruffled surface of their best behavior the two couples make moves and countermoves, thrusts and counterthrusts, jockey for position, align and realign their forces, attack and retreat and, when expedient to do so, humbug both victory and defeat.

Such diabolic maneuvering is a typical Jamesian response to a situation that by its very nature seems to allow of no other alternative, so cruelly does it limit the possibilities for spontaneous action, which is one of his implicit measures of spiritual health. We spoke earlier of the mathematics of narrowing alternatives in the case of Kate Croy, and of the paralysis descending upon Merton in his reluctant involvement with Kate's plan, until his only safety lay in taking no step whatsoever; and yet there finally was no distinction, for his essential guilt, between acting and not acting.

And the situation is the same in *The Golden Bowl* too, except that at the end Maggie cannot rally even with a gesture, as Densher did (whatever one thinks of the gesture), or renounce the corruption that has involved her, protecting at least her lonely pride, as Milly and Strether each in his way did. Yet, even ignoring her passive role in helping to bring about the adultery, if we ask what other real option Maggie had once she became aware of the situation, we would be hard put to answer it. The alternative of open righteous indignation and direct confrontation of the guilty pair would allow her to preserve her integrity, but that is about all, for there is a direct conflict of interest between the moral and the emotional claims of her dilemma. This conflict is further complicated by the fact that she is trying not only to keep her husband but also to avoid the ultimate separation from her father. Tempted to tell him that their new grouping as a party of four has been arranged by Amerigo and Charlotte, who will "do everything in the world that suits us, save only one thing—prescribe a line for us that will make them separate," she seems to hear her father answer, "Separate, my dear? Do you want them to separate? Then you must want *us* to—you and me? For how can the one separation take place without the other?" And then she is haunted: "Say they accepted this account of their situation as a practical finality, acting upon it and proceeding to a division, would no sombre ghosts of the smothered past on either side show across the widening strait pale unappeased faces, or raise in the very passage deprecating denouncing hands?" (XXIV, 74). In the end, of course, this proves the only solution, but not without the suffering ghosts Maggie imagines. But the very attempt on her part to avoid this outcome is one of the things that make guile and deception a necessity: to keep up the brave front, to keep her father in ignorance, or apparent ignorance, to preserve the illusion of the *status quo* in the hopes that somehow in the end the illusion may transform itself into reality.

These requirements by their very nature preclude the free and open exercise of moral will. This is true whether one looks at Maggie's actions from the point of view of their motivation or their manner or their effect. However magnificent she tries to persuade herself she appears in her "blameless egoism," she is motivated by self-interest: to hold and keep what is precious to her regardless of who suffers. To accomplish this end she plunges into the deepest hypocrisy and without hesitation manipulates everyone on the horizon who can be of use to her. So she manipulates the chance guests who happen to be present at the last intimate meeting of her husband and Charlotte:

It was n't that she wished she had been of the remembered party and possessed herself of its secrets. . . . She could concern herself at present absolutely with no secret but her own. What occurred was simply that she became aware, at a stroke, of the quantity of further nourishment required by her own, and of the amount of it she might somehow extract from these people; whereby she rose of a sudden to the desire to possess and use them, even to the extent of braving, of fairly defying, of directly exploiting, or possibly quite enjoying, under cover of an evil duplicity, the felt element of curiosity with which they regarded her. (XXIV, 49)

So too Fanny, who is woven into the company by another of Maggie's "dissimulated arts":

She had her intense, her smothered excitements, some of which were almost inspirations; she had in particular the extravagant, positively at moments the amused, sense of *using* her friend to the topmost notch, accompanied with the high luxury of not having to explain. (XXIV, 144–145)

So too her father: "She was humbugging him already, by absolute necessity, as she had never never done in her life—doing it up to the full height of what she had allowed for . . . to prove there was nothing the matter with her" (XXIV, 79–80). Then it occurs to her that he might be of still further use: "She asked herself if it were n't thinkable, from the perfectly practical point of view, that she should simply sacrifice him" and that perhaps indeed he had arrived "just on purpose to *say* it to her himself in so many words: 'Sacrifice me, my own love; do sacrifice me, do sacrifice me!' Should she want to, should she insist on it, she might verily hear him bleating at her, all conscious and all accommodating, like some precious spotless exceptionally intelligent lamb" (XXIV, 82–83).

And sacrifice him she does finally, when there seems to be no other alternative; just as the Prince sacrifices Charlotte. So survival dictates the necessity for the compromises neither party was willing to make freely in the beginning, and the sad lesson learned is that they *are* a necessity. But there is no suggestion that happiness would have been purchased if the compromises had been freely made to begin with, only that considerable pain would have been avoided. James's last word again and again about "morality" comes to this: that its power lies in its capacity to prevent human beings from destroying one another as they inevitably do when they surrender it to gratify their blind yet brave hungers for pleasure. But pleasure itself is surrendered either way, and in the final analysis the choice lies between renunciation or destruction, partial capitulation or total loss.

The dramatic situations in these novels are in effect test cases of the most extreme sort, of a wide range of human capacities and possibilities that, in James's view, polarize themselves into the urge for gratification and the absolute necessity for curbing that urge, in spite of the sorrow and sense of emptiness, the ultimate frustration that that necessity entails. In this scheme itself there is nothing particularly new: it is close to the traditional Christian opposition between good and evil, in which "evil" has been understood precisely as the urge for gratification uncurbed and unchecked. The difference is in James's ultimate feelings and attitudes toward this opposition; and one feeling is very clearly regret that evil in this sense is *not* possible. This becomes particularly apparent when we consider the three "dark ladies," Madame de Vionnet, Kate Croy, and Charlotte Verver. All three are central images of desire and bear the full burden of responsibility for the temptation they represent. Their rivals, Mrs. Newsome, Milly, and Maggie, are pale yet dangerous shadows beside them; in their bravery, beauty, and magnificent sexuality the former group of women dominate their respective worlds in spite of their "immorality," and for this very fact pay a price. In the end each of them is expelled from the collective social organism like some noxious foreign body that by mistake gained entrance: Madame de Vionnet is abandoned, Kate rejected, Charlotte exiled. Each of their lovers, having sown his wild oats, returns to the fold, the home, or the society he had left for the sake of the woman, who now becomes some sort of a moral outlaw or scapegoat. Yet even in spite of this they dominate in the possibilities they have represented for energy and passion, and in the strength of their suffering, which is greater than that of their "pale lady" counterparts, since it is the suffering of someone who has loved and *been loved in return*.[27] So in the end even stern Strether can only think of Madame de Vionnet in terms of the "passion . . . mature, abysmal, pitiful" she represents, which is everything Strether's soul would have yearned for, had he been an undivided man. But self-division and irreconcilable ambivalence are as intimate to James's vision of life as they are to Strether's character, and so we get the peculiar effect in the novels of the burden of feeling and sympathy going to those characters who lie outside the pale of acceptability. It is not just because of their capacity for passion that they are

[27] So, at the hour of Charlotte's final desperation, Maggie imagines her crying out: "You don't know what it is to have been loved and broken with. You have n't been broken with, because in *your* relation what can there have been worth speaking of to break? Ours was everything a relation could be, filled to the brim with the wine of consciousness; and if it was to have no meaning, no better meaning than that such a creature as you could breathe upon it, at your hour, for blight, why was I myself dealt with all for deception? why condemned after a couple of short years to find the golden flame—oh, the golden flame!—a mere handful of black ashes?" (XXIV, 329–330).

rejected (though it is striking that the sexual attachments are all illicit), but because this very capacity gives them the power to hurt, to take, to manipulate, to possess, and to destroy. It is as if James in his compulsive tendency to see the world split in two, with half its goods on one side of an impassable barrier and half on the other, keeps seeking for someone or something that would finally reconcile the virtues of Milly Theale with the attractions of Kate Croy. But whatever his dream, his perception is that they are irreconcilable, and it is the elaboration of this perception finally to which his novels address themselves.

Maggie's place in this scheme is illuminating because she comes to represent the fusion of the negative attributes, not the positive, of James's polar vision of human nature, as if only the darker parts of man could finally cross the barrier, the white curtain, that divides him from himself. Her personality represents a union of what always were for James the destructive traits of the soul. Thus, in the exercise of the manipulative instincts, in pure will and sheer energy, she is at last more than Charlotte's equal, but she lacks Charlotte's beauty and charm and the power to stir and move others that James sees as somehow self-justifying, or potentially so in some dream world where that power could be placed on the side of the angels. But Maggie does not have this; furthermore, she loses the innocence, the freshness, the genuine humility that were her angelic if less potent virtues and becomes a receptacle for will alone, untempered by either animal beauty or divine. And so in some ways the last part of the book, under Maggie's sponsorship, resembles a sado-masochistic nightmare worthy of the dark dreams of Poe. The Prince and Charlotte, Fanny predicts, will be "mystified, confounded, tormented. But they won't *know*—and all their possible putting their heads together won't make them. That . . . will be their punishment. . . . It will be Maggie herself who will mete it out" (XXIV, 135–136). And for all that she loves Amerigo, even "wishes to spare him," it is just as an agent of torment and unholy retribution that she moves through the final pages. "It is you, cara, who are deep," he tells her helplessly when he capitulates to the combined power of her will and her beautiful fortune and collaborates with her in turning on Charlotte:

Instead of warning and advising he had reassured and deceived her; so that our young woman, who had been from far back, by the habit of her nature, as much on her guard against sacrificing others as if she felt the great trap of life mainly to be set for one's doing so, now found herself attaching her fancy to that side of the situation of the exposed pair which involved for themselves at least the sacrifice of the least fortunate. . . . She had hours of exaltation indeed when the meaning of all this pressed in upon her as a tacit vow from him to abide without question by whatever she should be able to achieve or think fit to prescribe. Then it was that even while holding her breath for the awe of it she truly felt almost able enough for anything. It was as if she had passed in a time incredibly short from being nothing for him to being all; it was as if . . . every turn of his head, every tone of his voice, in these days, *might* mean that there was but one way in which a proud man reduced to abjection could hold himself. (XXIV, 227–228)

There is of course no abstract scale of judgment by which we can measure the relative suffering of a woman betrayed against that of a woman sacrificed and a proud man reduced to abjection, but it becomes clearer and clearer in the course of the book that the Prince's anxiety, even terror, and Charlotte's anguish have absolute claims of their own and that the punishment, if only by compounding the mutual fear and pain, finally outweighs the crime. The real horror of Maggie's position is that she wants to destroy. So, moving among them, the false symbol of their "unimpaired beatitude,"

under that imputation, to her sense, they sat—the imputation of wondering, beneath and behind all their apparently straight play, if she were n't really watching them from her corner and consciously . . . holding them in her hand. She was asking herself at last how they could bear it . . . and the amount of enjoyed or at least achieved security represented by so complete a conquest of appearances was what acted on her nerves precisely with a kind of provocative force. She found herself for five minutes thrilling with the idea of the prodigious effect that, just as she sat there near them, she had at her command; with the sense that if she were but different—oh, ever so different!—all this high decorum would hang by a hair. There reigned for her absolutely during these vertiginous moments that fascination of the monstrous, that temptation of the horribly possible, which we so often trace by its breaking out suddenly, lest it should go further, in unexplained retreats and reactions. (XXIV, 232–233)

And she does retreat from that "provocation of opportunity which had assaulted her, within on her sofa, as a beast might have leaped at her throat" (XXIV, 235), from that "scene she might people, by the press of her spring, either with serenities and dignities and decencies, or with terrors and shames and ruins, things as ugly as those formless fragments of her golden bowl she was trying so hard to pick up" (XXIV, 236). But the reason she retreats is not moral revulsion, nor decency and dignity for their own sake, but the simple, selfish, and very human fear of losing the persons dearest to her heart: "The ways usually open to innocence outraged and generosity betrayed, would have been to give them up, and . . . giving them up was, marvelously, not to be thought of" (XXIV, 237).

The juxtapositions here between good and evil, truth and falsehood, are extraordinary. Maggie has reached the point, or the situation has reached the point, where, on the one hand, the simple act of telling the truth, of pointing the finger, making the straight accusation, would forever destroy everything that all of these people possess. Yet the temptation Maggie feels is not the temptation of truth for its own sake regardless of the consequences, but of destruction for its own sake regardless of its causes. On the other hand, the opposite temptation, to preserve dignity and serenity, can only be accomplished by maintaining the lie that nothing has happened, and for all that, what will really be saved is only the appearance, not the fact, of peace. But Maggie actually cares nothing at this point for the dubious claims of either truth or falsehood. She is moved by the conflicting desires to destroy these people and to keep them, and neither impulse has to do with morality or with "goodness." The truth will kill, the lie will save; or so she thinks.

And in so thinking Maggie breaks down the distinction between herself and the Prince once and for all. She has come full circle from faith in the reality of appearances to faith in their efficacy, a very different thing. Concomitant with this change is a shift in her fundamental attitudes toward and evaluation of the human soul, in that "extraordinary American good faith" in "the world, the beautiful world." If previously appearances were to be trusted because they were the outward reflection of this essential beauty of life, now her disillusion is complete and she feels only pain and horror: "the horror of finding evil seated all at its ease where she had only dreamed of good; the horror of the thing hideously *behind*, behind so much trusted, so much pretended, nobleness, cleverness, tenderness" (XXIV, 237).

She is as close now, as close as it is possible for this "agitated lamb" to be, to sharing her husband's vision that "everything's terrible, cara—in the heart of man." The difference is in her capacity to feel shock and horror over the discovery (which was never a discovery anyway for Amerigo but an inherited assumption of honorable antiquity) and in her continuing need to maintain the illusion of her own rectitude. To do so, recall, "She had always been capable of cutting down more or less her prior term," and that is what she does now: she arrives at a new definition of "the right," in which the prior terms are not only cut down but exactly reversed, and like the Prince and Charlotte before her she makes a holy mission out of the flawless preservation of appearances.

He had given her something to conform to [deceiving Charlotte], and she had n't unintelligently turned on him, "gone back on" him, as he would have said, by not conforming. They were together thus, he and she, close, close together—whereas Charlotte, though rising there radiantly before her, was really off in some darkness of space that would steep her in solitude and harass her with care. The heart of the Princess swelled accordingly even in her abasement; [28] she had kept in tune with the right, and something certainly, something that might resemble a rare flower snatched from an impossible ledge, would, and possibly soon, come of it for her. The right, the right—yes, it took this extraordinary form of humbugging, as she had called it, to the end. It was only a question of not by a hair's breadth deflecting into the truth. . . .

And she made a point even, our young woman, of not turning away . . . but she stood there for anything more and till the weight should be lifted. With which she saw soon enough what more was to come. She saw it in Charlotte's face, and felt it make between them, in the air, a chill that completed the coldness of their conscious perjury. "Will you kiss me on it then?" (XXIV, 250–251)

When the point has been reached at which "the right" and "the truth" are antithetical and perjury becomes the mainstay of morality, a corner has indeed been turned. The positive sanction, the conscious ethical principle, for Maggie in all this is not to "go back" on her husband, not, so to say, to tattle on him; in addition she is swept aloft by the feeling that it is now they who are together and Charlotte off alone, isolated and harassed in the darkness. So the mixture of motives persists, though tempered always by Maggie's sense that she is primarily moved by moral considerations (however she may define them at a given time), and that she is not to blame if certain fringe benefits accrue to her in the process: such as having her husband helpless in a new alliance with her, such as the anguished humiliation and solitude of her enemy.

And yet one of the strangest effects in the book is the

---

[28] The abasement of telling Charlotte that she accuses her of nothing, and that she has not been wronged by her.

way Maggie's capacity for compassion and human awareness enlarges side by side with a renewed self-deception
that is more than the equal of her initial unseeing
innocence. Assuring Fanny that in spite of the deception
being practiced upon her, Charlotte can if she wishes "get
at" Amerigo, and even "alone," it suddenly sweeps over
Maggie that "stated so simply, what was it but dreadful,
truly, that the feasibility of Charlotte's 'getting at' the
man who for so long had loved her should now be in
question?" (XXIV, 327). Similarly, she imagines Charlotte behind a hard glass, "frantically tapping, from
within, by way of supreme, irrepressible entreaty"—an
entreaty that Maggie translates as a piercing reminder
that she herself does not, cannot know "what it is to have
been loved and broken with." And where one moment she
exults over Amerigo's banishment of Charlotte into outer
darkness, the next moment finds her condemning him for
this very act: "He ought to wish to see her . . . he ought
to be ready, he ought to be happy, he ought to feel
himself sworn—little as it is for the end of such a
history!—to take from her. It's as if he wished to get off
without taking anything" (XXIV, 331). And she confesses
to Fanny that she is not "sure of him": "If I were sure of
him I should n't doubt . . . that he must feel how much
less than she he pays—and how that ought to keep her
present to him" (XXIV, 332).

Maggie has other, similar recognitions of Charlotte
caged and trapped, of Adam Verver turning, for his wife,
into a demonic little wizard in which "the likeness of their
connexion would n't have been wrongly figured if he had
been thought of as holding in one of his pocketed hands

the end of a long silken halter looped round her beautiful neck. He did n't twitch it, yet it was there; he did n't drag it, but she came" (XXIV, 287); of Charlotte at the end of that halter lecturing the guests on the inestimable value of a "baroque" specimen as she practices for her new profession, "that of representing the arts and the graces to a people languishing, afar off, in ignorance." Maggie listens, and the

high voice went on; its quaver was doubtless for conscious ears only, but there were verily thirty seconds during which it sounded, for our young woman, like the shriek of a soul in pain. Kept up a minute longer it would break and collapse—so that Maggie felt herself the next thing turn with a start to her father. "Can't she be stopped? Hasn't she done it *enough?*" (XXIV, 292)

The compassion is genuine: Maggie is weeping at this point, and she weeps again in her last conversation with Fanny when she tells her that nobody knows the extent of Adam's knowledge; "Nobody."

"Not—a little—Charlotte?"

"A little?" the Princess echoed. "To know anything would be, for her, to know enough."

"And she does n't know anything?"

"If she did," Maggie answered, "Amerigo would."

"And that's just it—that he does n't?"

"That's just it," said the Princess profoundly.

On which Mrs. Assingham reflected. "Then how is Charlotte so held?"

"Just *by* that."

"By her ignorance?"

"By her ignorance."

Fanny wondered. "A torment—?"

"A torment," said Maggie with tears in her eyes. (XXIV, 335–336)

One of the things that are happening to Maggie is that her feelings are being educated in spite of the various convolutions of her will. It must be kept in mind that her tears come barely a moment after she has told Fanny that she and Adam are more "lost" to each other than Charlotte and Amerigo are, "since for them it's just, it's right, it's deserved, while for us it's only sad and strange and not caused by our fault" (XXIV, 333). She is learning something about the inherent dignity and claim that mutual passion can have even when it is outside the laws of convention and kindness; she is also learning that even suffering that is "deserved" can pierce the heart. And to an extent this growth of awareness—very similar to Strether's —brings her a new dignity too, an added sense of the possible dimensions of sorrow.

But though her pity and compassion are real, the distortion her values have undergone persists. Her impulse is to be kind now to Charlotte, to do her some service. That in itself is not surprising: Maggie's human awareness *has* been enlarged, and at the same time there is real psychological truth in the notion that "if you would forgive your enemy, first do him an injury." It is the form Maggie's kindness takes that is the chilling thing: to deceive Charlotte and then to deceive her still more deeply. The kiss of perjury was not enough:

She not only now saw her companion fairly agree to take her then for the poor little person she was finding it so easy to appear, but fell, in a secret, responsive ecstasy, to wondering if there were n't some supreme abjection with which she might be inspired. Vague but increasingly brighter, this possibility glimmered on her. It at last hung there adequately plain to Charlotte that she had presented herself once more to (as they said) grovel; and that, truly, made the stage large. (XXIV, 313)

The groveling takes the form of allowing Charlotte to accuse her of having nearly ruined her stepmother's marriage by the "ugliness" of her attachment to her father. Maggie plays her scene to the hilt:

"You want to take my father *from* me?"
The sharp successful almost primitive wail in it made Charlotte turn, and this moment attested for the Princess the felicity of her deceit. Something in her throbbed as it had throbbed the night she stood in the drawing-room and denied that she had suffered. She was ready to lie again if her companion would but give her the opening. Then she should know that she had done all. (XXIV, 316)

This scene is a *tour de force* of masochistic self-manipulation and disguised sadism, the mixture of innocence in guilt and guilt in innocence, that dazzling curtain of white light that conceals the opposite of what it shows and in which "the irresponsible ferociousness of the creature stands invested in the fleece of celestial innocence and love." [29] Maggie, even at this point, is still innocent in the sense that she is unconscious of the cruelty that is hidden in the center of her personal humiliation and "supreme abjection." Her consciousness is the consciousness of the martyr and the saint, in which personal sacrifice is the paradoxical measure of personal

[29] *Moby-Dick*, p. 186 n.

triumph. But the sadism is real, and Maggie is a false saint; that is, she is much more human than she knows. And this is the case *even if we accept the inversion of her values* and the principle that "the truth" and "the right" are in this case antithetical, that the road to Heaven is paved with lies:

"And she did n't really know you at all. [This is the Prince speaking to Maggie.] She does n't know you now."

"Ah yes she does!" said Maggie.

But he shook his head—he knew what he meant. "She not only does n't understand you more than I, she understands you ever so much less. Though even I—!"

"Well, even you?" Maggie pressed as he paused.

"Even I, even I even yet—!" Again he paused and the silence held them.

But Maggie at last broke it. "If Charlotte does n't understand me, it's because I've prevented her. I've chosen to deceive her and to lie to her."

The Prince kept his eyes on her. "I know what you've chosen to do. But I've chosen the same."

"Yes," said Maggie after an instant—"my choice was made when I had guessed yours."

. . ."She's stupid," he abruptly opined.

"O-oh!" Maggie protested in a long wail.

It had made him in fact quickly change colour. "What I mean is that she's not, as you pronounce her, unhappy." And he recovered with this all his logic. "Why is she unhappy if she does n't know?"

"Does n't know—?" She tried to make his logic difficult.

"Does n't know that *you* know."

. . ."She knows, she knows!" Maggie proclaimed. (XXIV, 347–348)

And so by Maggie's own admission Charlotte has in fact *not* been deceived—she knows, if not everything, "enough"; and "besides . . . she does n't believe us." The kindness Maggie has performed for her thus reduces itself to the ambiguous charity of allowing her to save face, while having to know that she is being so allowed. Yet Charlotte must grope in the dark right to the end: no matter what she knows intuitively she is not to be *told*, Maggie makes this explicit, and her exile must take place under conditions of permanent uncertainty without the solace of a real farewell or confrontation with Amerigo, exchange of facts and settling of things. The beauty of this state of affairs from Maggie's point of view is that she can continue to pretend that her final vengeance on Charlotte is an act of compassion, protection, even love. This *is* the interpretation that follows from the premise that "the right, the right . . . was only a question of not, by a hair's breadth, deflecting into the truth."

It is a position that, like the Prince's bland historical sorrow ("Everything's terrible, cara—in the heart of man"), has a grotesque innocence of its own, more blinding than all the "extraordinary American good faith" on the entire continent. It is the innocence of the Roman arena and the pagan childhood of man; it is like an Eden where Cain slew Abel but was branded with no mark of shame and was not cast out. "The soul of drama," said James, "is catastrophe determined in spite of opposition"; like Milly, Maggie herself has been the opposition. Unlike Milly, the powers she used to resist were the powers of despair and experience: duplicity, deception, manipulation.

The Negative Imagination

The terms "good" and "evil" in such a context lose their meaning, become interchangeable and therefore in an ultimate sense "absurd." And morally this book is absurd. Yet it has a persistent, haunting beauty, a beauty of form, of imagery; the shape of a dance dreamed by a man who, through a strange alchemy in the "workshop of his brain," transformed his negative imaginings into the positive triumph of art. Moreover, in a certain sense the absurdity is the whole point, for it is precisely the arbitrary reign of consciousness that James's work celebrates: the capacity of human mind to establish new conventions, change the significance of words, cut down its "prior term," make and unmake meanings, both reflecting and creating itself in its supreme fictions.

Bibliography

Auerbach, Erich. *Mimesis: The Representation of Reality in Western Literature*, trans. Willard Trask. Garden City, New York, 1957. Doubleday & Co., Inc.

Bersani, Leo. "From Bachelard to Barthes," *Partisan Review*, XXXIV (Spring, 1967), 215–232.

——"Variations on a Paradigm," *New York Times Book Review* (June 11, 1967), 6, 45.

Bewley, Marius. *The Eccentric Design: Form in the Classic American Novel*. New York, 1963. Columbia University Press.

Blackmur, R. P. Introduction to *The Golden Bowl*. New York, 1952. Pp. v–xxi. Grove Press.

Booth, Wayne. *The Rhetoric of Fiction*: Chicago, 1962. The University of Chicago Press.

Brower, Reuben. *The Fields of Light: An Experiment in Critical Reading*. New York, 1951. Oxford University Press.

Bibliography

Camus, Albert. *The Stranger,* trans. Stuart Gilbert. New York, 1946. Alfred A. Knopf, Inc.

Chase, Richard. "James' *Ambassadors.*" *Twelve Original Essays on Great American Novels,* ed. Charles Shapiro. Detroit, 1958. Pp. 124–127. Wayne State University Press.

Dupee, F. W. *Henry James.* Garden City, New York, 1956. Doubleday & Co., Inc.

——, ed. *The Question of Henry James: A Collection of Critical Essays.* New York, 1945. H. Holt and Company.

Edel, Leon. *Henry James: The Conquest of London, 1870–1881.* Philadelphia, New York, 1962. J. B. Lippincott Co.

——. *Henry James: The Middle Years, 1882–1895.* Philadelphia, New York, 1962. J. B. Lippincott Co.

——. *Henry James: The Untried Years, 1843–1870.* Philadelphia, New York, 1953. J. B. Lippincott Co.

Ellmann, Richard, and Charles Feidelson, Jr., eds. *The Modern Tradition: Backgrounds of Modern Literature.* New York, 1965. Oxford University Press.

Foucault, Michel. *Madness and Civilization: A History of Insanity in the Age of Reason,* trans. Richard Howard. New York, 1965. Random House, Inc.

Genet, Jean. *The Screens,* trans. Bernard Frechtman. New York, 1962. Grove Press.

Gide, André. *The Journals of André Gide, 1889–1949, I: 1889–1924, II: 1924–1949,* trans. Justin O'Brien. New York, 1956. Vintage Books, Inc.

Goode, John. "Character and Henry James," *New Left Review,* No. 40 (November–December 1966), 55–75.

Hawthorne, Nathaniel. *A Wonder Book.* Garden City, New York, no date. Garden City Publishing Co., Inc.

Hueffer, Ford Madox. *Henry James: A Critical Study.* New York, 1916. Dodd, Mead & Company.

James, Alice. *The Diary of Alice James,* ed. Leon Edel. New York, 1964. Dodd, Mead & Company.

Bibliography

James, Henry. *The Art of the Novel: Critical Prefaces,* ed. R. P. Blackmur. New York, 1962. Charles Scribner's Sons.

———. *Autobiography of Henry James: A Small Boy and Others; Notes of a Son and Brother; The Middle Years,* ed. F. W. Dupee. New York, 1956. Criterion Books, Inc.

———. *The Europeans: A Sketch.* London, 1952. John Lehmann Ltd.

———. *French Poets and Novelists.* New York, 1904. Macmillan & Co.

———. *Literary Reviews and Essays: On American, English and French Literature,* ed. Albert Mordell. New York, 1957. Grove Press.

———. *The Notebooks of Henry James,* ed. F. O. Matthiessen and Kenneth B. Murdock. New York, 1955. George Braziller, Inc.

———. *The Novels and Tales of Henry James: New York Edition.* 24 vols. New York, 1907–1909. Charles Scribner's Sons. (Two volumes were added posthumously.)

———. *The Sacred Fount.* New York, 1953. Grove Press.

———. *The Selected Letters of Henry James,* ed. Leon Edel. New York, 1955. Farrar, Straus and Cudahy.

Joyce, James. *The Critical Writings of James Joyce,* eds. Ellsworth Mason and Richard Ellmann. New York, 1959. The Viking Press, Inc.

Lawrence, D. H. *Studies in Classic American Literature.* Garden City, New York, 1953. Doubleday & Company, Inc.

Leavis, F. R. *The Great Tradition.* Garden City, New York, 1954. Doubleday & Company, Inc.

Marcus, Steven. *The Other Victorians: A Study of Sexuality and Pornography in Mid-Nineteenth-Century England.* New York, 1966. Basic Books, Inc.

Matthiessen, F. O. *Henry James: The Major Phase.* New York, 1944. Oxford University Press.

Bibliography

Maugham, W. Somerset. *The Vagrant Mood: Six Essays.* London, 1952. William Heinemann Ltd.

Melville, Herman. *Moby-Dick: Or the Whale.* New York, 1953. Rinehart & Co., Inc.

Murdoch, Iris, "The Sublime and the Beautiful Revisited," *The Yale Review* (December 1959), 241–271.

Nuhn, Ferner. *The Wind Blew from the East: A Study in the Orientation of American Culture.* New York, 1940.

Ortega y Gasset, José. *The Dehumanization of Art and Other Writings on Art and Culture.* Garden City, New York, 1956. Doubleday & Company, Inc.

Rahv, Philip. *Image and Idea.* Norfolk, Connecticut, 1957. A New Directions Paperback.

Robbe-Grillet, Alain. *For a New Novel: Essays on Fiction,* trans. Richard Howard. New York, 1965. Grove Press, Inc.

Rosenberg, Harold. *The Tradition of the New.* New York, 1961. Grove Press, Inc.

Smith, James Harry and Edd Winfield Parks, eds., 3d ed., *The Great Critics: An Anthology of Literary Criticism.* New York, 1951. W. W. Norton & Company, Inc.

Sontag, Susan. "The Pornographic Imagination," *Partisan Review,* XXXIV (Spring, 1967), 181–212.

Spender, Stephen. *The Destructive Element: A Study of Modern Writers and Beliefs.* London, 1935.

Stoll, Elmer Edgar. "Give the Devil His Due," *Review of English Studies,* XX (April 1944), 108–124.

Trilling, Lionel. Introduction to *The Princess Casamassima.* New York, 1948. Pp. v–xlviii. The Macmillan Company.

Warren, Austin. *Rage for Order: Essays in Criticism.* Ann Arbor, Michigan, 1959. The University of Michigan Press.

Wharton, Edith. *A Backward Glance.* New York, 1934. Charles Scribner's Sons.

Willen, Gerald, ed., *A Casebook on Henry James's "The Turn of the Screw.*" New York, 1960. Thomas Y. Crowell Company.

Woolf, Virginia. *The Common Reader: First Series.* New York, 1925. Harcourt, Brace and Company.

Index of Names and Titles

Acton, William, 13
Ambassadors, The, 5–6, 10, 88, 101–151, 155–160, 163–164, 169–170, 185–187, 189, 191, 193, 199, 208–209, 218; Preface, 118, 122–123
American, The, 3–4, 62; Preface, 4, 147–148
"Art of Fiction, The," 35, 51
"Aspern Papers, The," 33
Auerbach, Erich, 21, 38, 49
Austen, Jane, 108
Autobiography: A Small Boy and Others; Notes of a Son and Brother; The Middle Years, 27, 124–125
Awkward Age, The, 17, 76, 87, 130, 191

Bachelard, Gaston, 34
Barthes, Roland, 34
Baudelaire, Charles, 48–50, 186
"Beast in the Jungle, The," 133, 156

Beckett, Samuel, 34
Bennett, Arnold, 43, 47
Berg, Jean de (pseudonym), 27
Bersani, Leo, 34, 42
Blackmur, R. P., 45, 169, 170, 186
Blake, William, 124
Booth, Wayne, 29–30, 33, 36–37
Bostonians, The, 120, 130, 134, 157
Brontës, the, 39
Brower, Reuben, 90
Burroughs, William, 37, 45

Camus, Albert, 44, 52–57
Chase, Richard, 108, 121
Conrad, Joseph, 47

"Daisy Miller," 191
Dickens, Charles, 39
Dreiser, Theodore, 162, 166
du Bos, Charles, 48
Dumas, Alexandre, 44

Index

Edel, Leon, 6, 48
Eliot, T. S., 129
Europeans, The: A Sketch, xii, 5–12, 15, 16, 62

Faulkner, William, 51, 129, 190
Flaubert, Gustave, 34, 49–50, 132
Foucault, Michel, 14
French Poets and Novelists, 48–49
Freud, Sigmund, 14

Galsworthy, John, 47
Genet, Jean, 45, 54–55
Gide, André, 18, 45, 47–48, 74–75
Golden Bowl, The, xi, xiii, 17, 29, 35, 45, 50, 89, 101, 107–108, 120, 128, 130, 132–134, 146–147, 150–151, 155–222; Preface, 173–174, 181–186
Goncourt, Edmond de, 48–49
Goode, John, 41
Gosse, Edmund, 50

Hardy, Thomas, 18, 47, 56
Hawthorne, Nathaniel, 48–49, 87, 129, 144, 167, 180
Hemingway, Ernest, 48, 129
Howells, William Dean, 105
Hueffer, Ford Madox, 89

Ibsen, Henrik, 102

James, Alice, 14
Joyce, James, 48, 51, 129

Keats, John, 124, 167
Kermode, Frank, 42

Lawrence, D. H., 87, 129
Leavis, F. R., 45, 83, 88–89, 132, 184–186
Letters of Henry James, 6; to Rhoda Broughton, 55; to Godkin, 50; to Edmund Gosse, 50; to William Roughhead, 55
Literary Reviews and Essays: On American, English, and French Literature, 49–51

Longfellow, Henry Wadsworth, 87
Loring, Katharine Peabody, 14

Maeterlinck, Maurice, 102
Marcus, Steven, 13–14
Marvell, Andrew, 127
Matthiessen, F. O., xii, 74–75, 121, 124, 161
Maugham, W. Somerset, 132
Melville, Herman, 180, 194–196, 219
Molière, 108
Montaigne, Michel, 169
Murdoch, Iris, 40–41

Notebooks, The, 93, 105
Nuhn, Ferner, 173, 192

Ortega y Gasset, José, 41–43, 51, 55, 126

Poe, Edgar Allan, 48–49, 87, 129, 167, 180, 194, 211
Portrait of a Lady, The, xi, 19, 66, 83–84, 89, 120–121, 129–131, 133, 146–148, 150–151, 166, 191; Preface, 19–20, 122
Prefaces: The Ambassadors, 118, 122–123; The American, 4, 147–148; The Golden Bowl, 173–174, 181–186; The Portrait of a Lady, 19–20, 122; Roderick Hudson, 26, 44, 131–132; The Tragic Muse, 44; What Maisie Knew, 18, 21–30; The Wings of the Dove, 56–57, 63–67, 73, 80, 83
Princess Casamassima, The, 136, 191
Proust, Marcel, 21, 51

Rahv, Philip, 162
Réage, Pauline (pseudonym), 27
Robbe-Grillet, Alain, 34, 41, 45, 51–53, 180
Roderick Hudson, 17, 26, 62; Preface, 26, 44, 131–132
Rosenberg, Harold, 47

Sacred Fount, The, xi, 17, 25, 35–37, 54–55, 76, 156, 159, 177–178

Sartre, Jean-Paul, 44–45, 52–53, 180

Shakespeare, William, 103, 121, 132

Sontag, Susan, 45–46

Spender, Stephen, 185

Stoll, Elmer Edgar, 95

Tolstoy, Leo, 43, 44, 46, 132

Trilling, Lionel, 136–137

Turn of the Screw, The, 17, 35, 75, 156

Warren, Austin, 48, 102

Washington Square, 87, 191

Watts, Ian, 36

Wells, H. G., 40, 43, 45, 47

Wharton, Edith, 40, 47

What Maisie Knew, xii–xiii, 17–18, 20, 22–34, 37, 76, 87; Preface, 18, 21–30

Whitman, Walt, 179

Wilde, Oscar, 50

Wilson, Edmund, 17–19, 25, 35

Wings of the Dove, The 62–98, 102, 108, 120, 128–129, 133–134, 146–147, 149–151, 155, 157–159, 163–164, 166–167, 169–171, 185, 187–189, 191, 193, 205, 208–210, 221; Preface, 56–57, 63–67, 73, 80, 83

Woolf, Virginia, 37–38, 47, 51

Yeats, W. B., 124

"Younger Generation, The," 43